The Intruder
a love story

BRETT SHAPIRO

with selected correspondence
of Giovanni Forti

atmosphere press

© 2025 Brett Shaprio

Published by Atmosphere Press

Cover design by Felipe Betim

Originally published in Italy by Giangiacomo Feltrinelli Editore in 1993.

No part of this book may be reproduced without permission from the author except in brief quotations and in reviews.

Atmospherepress.com

Praise for *The Intruder*
Acclaim from the Italian Release

"A tale of love that transcends the agony of death. A private story that becomes public and exemplary."
— *Il Mattino* (Titta Fiore)

"A passionate and intense love story that must contend not only with deeply ingrained prejudices but also with an impending tragedy. These pages leave no room for sentimentality; instead, they recount, with a clarity born of true emotion and reason, the upheavals caused by an intruder within a family that, in its domestic organization, division of roles, and affection for its children, mirrors the portrait of many heterosexual couples."
— *Rocca* (Stefano Cazzaro)

"A raw and honest book, laying bare the nerves and emotions. It unsettles, provokes...and disheartens."
— *Il Resto del Carlino* (Gianni Gennasi)

"A challenge to our ever-present moral complacency, a slap in the face to prejudice, a call to open-mindedness... This book doesn't just move us with the account of Giovanni's slow decline and Brett's unwavering, passionate devotion to his partner's fate—it shakes us to the core with stark, unembellished truth."
— *Il Giornale di Vicenza* (Alida Airaghi)

"It would be limiting to read this book solely as a testimony. It is that, of course, but not only that. It is a lucid reportage, carried out with a sharp awareness—not the awareness that comes 'after,' when all that remains is to take stock and salvage whatever is left of life, but the awareness of someone who, from the very beginning, 'knows' the ending rationally (having already seen it written in the identical fate of others—acquaintances, friends, lovers) and yet, just as rationally, refuses to yield even an inch. Not even at the very end, when the temptation to shorten the suffering of the beloved companion is at its strongest. [...] More than anything, this is a book about love, pain, and death, which, in this case, does not at all coincide with the end of love."

— *Essepiu* (Scaffale)

"Giovanni's letters are framed by Brett's narratives—calm, profound, and elegant; a love story intertwined with two historically significant elements: a same-sex marriage, lived and recounted with complete naturalness, and the scourge of an epidemic. But above all, it is a story of love and living. The energy and enthusiasm that radiate from the body and mind of a young adult—allowing him to be a professional, a husband, a parent, a son, a brother, a friend, and an engaged citizen both politically and culturally—permeate the entire book, even as they begin to fade with the onset of illness."

— *Il Gazzettino* (Elena Bignami)

"Entering the second millennium, AIDS finds images to narrate itself. Through real-time chronicles that read like unflinching clinical reports, it has found the words to be spoken—bitter, unrelenting words. Words that burn, exposing the trajectory of a disease whose scandalous visibility lays bare social relationships, fear, and shame. Yet, it also confers a harrowing stature upon artists and writers. One thing is certain: This immense suffering, paired with an indomitable force, has given rise to unprecedented situations—inscrutable and entirely unknown to humanity until just a few years ago. These are described with restraint and a tenderness that brings one to the brink of tears in the epistolary narrative *L'Intruso* (*The Intruder*). The story recounts the battle between illness and life, exploring how its protagonists—without any precedents or reference points—have forged new meanings of fatherhood, spirituality, and family. Each already has a child, and together, after officially marrying, they long to adopt another in their desperate hope, as if such an excess of kindness, tenderness, and vitality might somehow triumph over the virus."

— *Elle* (Giuse Ferre)

"The unwavering presence of someone beside a loved one in their final moments is nothing new in human experience. The worst illnesses, harbingers of death, have always been met with love's unyielding resistance. We see it in mothers, in the extraordinary devotion of countless sensitive souls, in the saints who care for the sick with boundless charity. But here, it is a gay man standing by his partner. It feels like witnessing the heart-wrenching unfolding of an impossible myth: love that transcends and triumphs over the monstrosity of suffering; love that seeks to bridge the chasm between life and death; love that dares to stand equal in magnitude."
– *Gli altri: che farne* (Furio Colombo)

"Impossible to reach the end without crying."
– *Corriere della Sera* (Gianni Riotta)

Praise for *Late in the Day*

"...a deeply affecting book, not just about the fear of aging, but also the need for human connection in the face of mortality. A ruminative and moving exploration of friendship and death."
– *Kirkus Reviews*

"The author has the ability to penetrate the depths of the human psyche ...and the light and energy that pulls humanity forward through shared experience... The writing is gorgeous, lyrical, and infused with realism...you'll love Shapiro's beguiling prose, the finesse in humor, the exceptionally written characters, and the dazzling portrait of companionship at the dusk of life."
– *The Book Commentary*

"Brett Shapiro delivers a heartfelt read by uniting three unsuspecting souls in his latest novel... [He] has done a masterful job of marrying the stand-alone lives of three people who would eventually merge together into a wonderful journey of life itself. He has an exceptional vision."
– *Feathered Quill*

Praise for *Those around Him*

"The many metaphorical forays into hurricane season and the intensity of well-crafted literary writing bring what could have been a quiet, unnoticeable story into brilliant, thoughtful focus."

– US Review of Books

"...a story about five people who are totally different characters, but they all have one thing in common - their anger against their upbringing, their parents, siblings, and the world...This is a book that has to be read."

– Readers' Favorite

"...a lyrical meditation on living in the middle ground – between past and future, youth and age, duty and desire. In language that captures the rush and flow of thought, the reader is carried along on Andrew's journey and reconciliation as he endeavors to make peace with the relentless march of time. His story is intimate, authentic and unforgettable."

– Rachel Hyde, author of More Than We Know

ALSO BY BRETT SHAPIRO

Henry's Version

Late in the Day

Those around Him

Bailey Strikes It Rich
(in French, German and Korean only)

The Adventures of Bailey the Bag Dog
(in French and German only)

Nourishing the Land, Nourishing the People
(also in French)

Regenerating Forests and Livelihoods

Preface

by Rossana Rossanda (1993)[1]

This is a love story from the end of our century. As overwhelming as the presence of an illness like AIDS may be—still synonymous with death—it is not the story of an agony. And as poignant as the evocation of a young man, whom many of us have known, may be, it is not a portrait. It is the narration of a love relationship that has both given and asked, and the two moments cannot be separated, not even when the giving of one to the other prevails. Because in both, love remains a need.

Brett Shapiro and Giovanni Forti meet in 1990 on seemingly equal footing. Both have lost a partner—not because of illness, but because a passion can come to an end. Both have a child, who, despite not being biological, is even more of a child to them—wanted and won. Both are intellectuals in a moment of solitude—perhaps more familiar to Brett, while for Giovanni, it is the result of the end of a youth deeply committed to political engagement and not exhausted by professional success.

Brett is American; Giovanni is Italian, somewhat apart

---

[1] Rossana Rossanda was one of Italy's leading journalists, politicians and feminists. Giovanni Forti was guided by her during his long stint at *il manifesto*, an Italian left-wing daily newspaper. La Rossanda died in 2020. She was 96 years old.

from the community of foreign journalists in New York—a world from which something has distanced him. Brett is not ill, and Giovanni is convinced he isn't either.

He is HIV positive but not sick, or so he believes. He believes he will never become ill. Should he be the only one, the first, he will be the first to escape seropositivity, he thinks and says. Certainly, he isn't the only one who, already sick, thought this way: if for everyone it is inconceivable to imagine their own end with AIDS—slow, stealthy, absurd in its origin, tortuous in its remissions—the structured self genuinely tends to believe that the immune defenses (what do they consist of, how do they position themselves between materiality and psyche, what idea of the body do they suggest?) are a zone over which consciousness can exert influence.

Thus, Giovanni, when he seeks and meets Brett, wants to love and be loved "forever," as love always says to itself. If he immediately reveals his condition to Brett, it is out of honesty rather than precaution or fear; that Brett accepts him with tenderness becomes an additional bond, a shared secret, a vital specificity of their relationship.

The asymmetry will soon become unavoidable. Giovanni has doubled down on life and will continue to do so even when he is already very unwell, and Brett is the first to notice. One believes himself to be asymptomatic despite all evidence to the contrary, while the other cannot deceive himself. But how can they say it to each other? The gaze between the two is no longer equal. Nor is their mutual demand, their expectation.

Giovanni will reluctantly acknowledge his exhaustion, a decline from which there is no recovery. Only too late does the end become clear to him—not knowing when, but horribly premature—premature, premature, the two men obsessively repeat to themselves, convinced that for the elderly, decline and death, being "natural," are somehow "acceptable." But from that moment, Giovanni slips into the solitude of someone who feels they can no longer communicate the essential—the fact that they feel themselves dying—to someone alive, who, like all the living, is disproportionately full of life, oblivious, and wasteful with that life, which for Giovanni is slipping through his fingers like water. Suddenly, the sick person's credit toward the world seems infinite, yet the world remains deaf and inadequate. Giovanni is left with silence—not because he has nothing to say; he has everything to scream—but because no one can truly hear him.

From then on, Giovanni's feelings toward Brett, who cares for him like no one else, become a mixture of love—fading, as life fades—and irritation and pity, because he sees Brett suffering through the immense effort, and he sees it as insufficient (everything is insufficient, the sick person tells himself, nothing is enough, perhaps more could have been done).

And Brett understands, he feels it. Giovanni's descent into an illness that spares no part of the body, and the overwhelming priority that his shattered body takes over his consciousness, means not only that Brett is losing the man he loves, but also that Brett himself is increasingly lost to Giovanni. He occupies less and less space, becomes less and less significant to the other, and, as happens when one loves, is almost erased and returned to himself as if by cancellation.

What do we seek in love if not reassurance: "You are essential to me; you must exist because, without you, I would not be." This soothes our uncertainty. Brett cannot help but seek this answer because he is not an assistant; he is a lover, and as long as a glimmer of light remains, he needs to hear it repeated to him. At the cost of beating his head against the wall, he cries out in despair in Giovanni's final days: "I'm here with you, you still love me and need me, right?"

"Am I necessary?" From Giovanni, the answer will come,

distant but clear: "No." It is the only true answer, but for a lover, it is devastating, demolishing—regardless of whatever remedy the psychoanalyst of the moment might try to administer. Someone who is dying clings, like a shell to a rock beneath the stormy sea, to that primary self, which is the perception of having come into existence and being alive before and after every relationship with the other. In this primordial and perhaps ultimate zone, the other does not exist.

And Brett plunges into the solitude of the living. At no point—this is his strength as a man and a writer—does he deny his frustration, reduce himself to being merely a compassionate hand, or find satisfaction in self-sacrificing devotion. Brett critiques, protests, struggles, and demands that the promise they made together—to be together forever, in good times and in bad—be honored when the bad times come. As Giovanni gradually withdraws from him—first in the division of responsibilities in their shared life and caring for the children, then in attentiveness, passion, or even just physical tenderness, and finally in time itself, as the sick man slips into sleep, longer and longer hours of sleep, retreating into his own enclosure—Brett suffers but also becomes furious. Giovanni tries to ward off the illness by throwing himself into dreams: he wants another child, he wants to return to Rome, he wants a house, assuming that Brett and Zach will come with him, breaking all ties with their current world. Brett counters the illness with the principle of reality: he responds to Giovanni as a whole person, alive and responsible, reproaching him for wanting too much and giving too little, shaking him from his surrender, which is truly the relinquishment of love to an unspeakable fatigue.

In this story, which is also a story of shared richness, the most heartrending pages are not those of the end but those of the marriage. Both had wanted it—not as a provocation, though knowing Giovanni, perhaps there was a hint of that—

but as a turn toward a fully shared existence, sealed by ritual. It wasn't easy to arrange for its celebration, and by the time they finally succeeded, Giovanni was already so unwell that the essential challenge was simply standing upright during what was meant to be a ceremony overflowing with mutual symbols and values. Standing with composure and a smile until, in the confusion of the congratulations, he could slip away to the nearest room and collapse into sleep on a couch, alone, to recover. And then, the night at the Carlyle, the honeymoon tenderly and playfully planned and prepared, with Giovanni exhausted by the effort, Brett by sadness and desire, both of them acutely aware of the infinite poverty of the other. This is love.

Afterward, the hardest part with himself will fall to Giovanni, and the hardest part with the other will fall to Brett. Already lost, Giovanni wants to adopt another child because he will have less of his own, who will have to spend part of his time with his mother. He dreams of a little girl, the other gender that has been fundamental in all his emotional experiences except for his sexuality. It falls to Brett to tell him that he cannot—that he is not in a position to provide a future for himself or for a child who would be entrusted to him. It's like delivering a blow, and Giovanni feels it, not without some resentment, as happens every time he makes plans. Plans for New York or for Rome, almost as if to challenge the other, to force Brett or his own mother to tell him that no, it cannot happen. Terrible to say, terrible to hear. This too is love: the kind that delivers blows and receives them.

...

But if love is its eternal paradigm, the story of Brett and Giovanni belongs to this century. Certainly because it is dominated by AIDS, which twenty years ago was unknown to us—a disease both invincible and, moreover, tied to an unforgiven transgression. Giovanni perceives it this way too and feels its double blow: in the idea of a boundless possibility of salvation, and in a boundless personal freedom. In ten or twenty years, AIDS will cease to be invincible, its paths will change, and an archaeologist will date a story like this without error.

Its precise placement in time extends far beyond the illness. Brett and Giovanni are both children of 1968 in the Western world—and only of 1968. That year touched other generations as well, coloring them, but they were already and would remain distinct. For many young people, especially students who were already freed from their fathers' ties, 1968 was the door flung open to the search for another meaning, through an unlimited experimentation that was, first and foremost, a reclaiming of the self. It was not a generation primarily focused on the world or characterized by solidarity, unlike the political generations that had preceded it. Its journey more closely resembles that of Prince Tamino in *The Magic Flute*—without a Sarastro and without an object to conquer other than the possession of oneself as happiness, a concept equally rare in modern consciousness.

For young people like them, the break was immense. Borders—once formidable—of culture, states, and sex suddenly ceased to exist, all joyfully to be dismantled, like any binding obligation to others. Not out of denial, but because the other was felt, as never before, to be a self-contained being, a separate continent. When the hope fell from that "revolution" of theirs, a society transformed by it, what remained was that perception of the self, and in some measure, it revealed itself to be its essential fruit.

For those of us who experienced 1968, as I did, from an already mature perspective, and saw it as the culmination of other imperfect revolutions, it was, for a time, surprising how the "'68-ers" could let that immense project slip away from themselves without much sense of loss; how, in fact, they sometimes recall it with annoyance. Giovanni doesn't remember it at all: he had worked with us on [the weekly Italian newspaper] il *manifesto*; on some occasions, he drove me mad whenever I met and clashed with him and others like him. But he was a multiplier of my questions, unforgettable.

For him, no: il *manifesto*, me, those of us who also lived through 1968 and shared decisive years with Giovanni are not part of his memory, not within the framework his memory provides. Of the journey we traveled together, what remains is an imprint of "the left," the non-pietistic rejection of poverty and war, the refusal to delude ourselves with easy successes. But the essential element is something else—it's the transformation of the relationship with oneself, just as for us, the essential element had been the transformation of the relationship with the world. We do not hold, for Giovanni's peers, the importance they held for us. And it's no coincidence that they went their own separate ways, even apart from one another.

Along that path, they did not settle, at least not the most coherent among them, those who did not retreat into compromise. For Giovanni, the discovery and then the affirmation of his sexual preference would not be lived as something separate from the rest of his life, nor as its dark and cursed side, as it had been in the great transgressive tradition of the early 20th century. Instead, it is a path no different from that of heterosexual relationships—determinative in existence and relationships, with the added sharp flavor of that degree of challenge that still, albeit less and less in an educated environment, it entails.

Above all, this order of relationships prioritizes the idea that nothing is obvious, nothing is already set on rails or transmitted. Happily chosen: his love for his young friends, a profession embraced with interest but at a distance—a good distance, once his work was well done—a country where he decided to live, a parenthood that was not obligatory, and family life. In the end, even his returns would be chosen, like the return to Judaism, to his family of origin, to the city of his youth.

This kind of path belongs to the 1970s. It did not exist before, and I am not sure if it will exist after. It also gives familiar categories—profession, parenthood, family, religion—a different meaning from what we, in our youth, had known and what we had vigorously freed ourselves from. It is a rediscovery unique to that generation, which did not belong to ours, and it appears innovative and problematic.

Above all, it is the rediscovery of conjugal love compared to love-passion and its transgressive sense—because even Giovanni fell into what he calls "excess," to which he unhesitatingly attributes his infection. But for Brett and him, love as a free contract of life is essential; so is marriage and family, rediscovered at the end of a journey rather than found behind them.

They meet through an ad that Brett, solitary and doubtful, places in a newspaper, which begins with the words: "Do you know how to change a diaper?" It means: are you seeking, besides me, a child—and in the fullest sense, that until yesterday was the domain of women—namely, a being to care for entirely for years, with effort and the obligations that childhood care entails?

These young men experience diapers, preparing food, schedules dictated by the needs of the child—therefore constrained and limited for themselves—even before the infinite questions about what to do and say, and how, which raising a human child requires. The female presence has slipped seamlessly out of their daily lives because, for them, it is natural—as it had never been in the history of men—to accept the "care work" or reproductive work, which, no longer felt as destiny, surprisingly appears rich.

Not less burdensome, sometimes exhausting, than what has been denounced by emancipation or feminism, which we all have experienced as far too real, but certainly, for a young man like Brett, no more unbearable than the other commitments an adult knows. Neither he nor Giovanni feels hindered by it in their self-realization. And it should be noted that they carry out domestic care under the not-so-simple conditions most women face, that is, alongside external work and without consistent domestic help. Having a child, creating a family, living together, sharing expenses and efforts—this is a choice for them, fulfilling a need.

What need? It's difficult to ask, for a woman like me. The answer does not come easily. Is it a substitute for the lack of a community once dreamed of in other years, now fallen, perhaps forgotten? But if that distant dream can be filled by a chosen family, does it not mean that the community was imagined as a place of relationships between individuals, men and women—not a society or a polis, but a relationship between the self and the other, constitutive of the self and self-sufficient? Brett simply says that it is about living not just love but "responsibility," meaning a demanding life project—this is, for him, the encounter with Giovanni and the children. It is not clear how much of that is also for Giovanni, in whom, as the time remaining for him diminishes, the priority of the relationship fades. Yet, for him too, the meeting with Brett is the meeting with a "life partner," with whom to build a non-transitory future, as well as with the adopted child. In comparison to the importance of this commitment, the bond of blood becomes entirely secondary and meaningless. What matters is the mutual pact—very binding, very egalitarian—between two young men forming a family with two children, to whom they propose themselves unequivocally as fathers. The equality of roles is beyond question. If, by chance, it is questioned—perhaps due to some domestic shortcoming—it causes a storm that brings them back to the shared responsibilities. Brett eventually becomes the one who cooks and cleans the house, but only because Giovanni is getting increasingly unwell: it goes without saying that Giovanni should be doing the same tasks and ensuring the household's order, as the lives of three other people are inscribed in his existence.

This family has no precedent in heterosexuality. At the same time, it retrieves the concrete and symbolic values of the codified image of the heterosexual family as the primary and reciprocal community. I repeat: a codified image rather than an experience, since for a brief period and not for everyone, the relationship between spouses was devoid of an implicit hierarchy. Even the love and physical passion between them acquire an unusual dynamic, perhaps as a form of compensation for the earlier "excess."

In this aspect, and for a woman, Brett Shapiro's book is surprising Certainly unusual, perhaps very American: as if this rediscovery-reconstruction of personal relationships belonged—like certain films also suggest—more to other societies than to ours. The testimony left to us by the Frenchman Hervé Guibert about his love/passion with his partner, also infected, is far less novel; they are two lovers, and the family is that of one of them, traditionally. Their passion, in many respects, appears fatal. Certainly, from Giovanni and Brett's experience emerges an unusual reflection on the possible nature of a familial relationship: it is not paradoxical that this relationship appears as wealth and self-fulfillment only insofar as it is entirely chosen. What is paradoxical is that it seems entirely and radically chosen only within a homosexual family. The heterosexual family, in fact, carries the burden of roles fixed over centuries and, perhaps for this reason, is never entirely chosen.

The innovation in meaning seems, moreover, stronger in the couple's relationship than in that between father and child.

Even if the father, in Brett's case, embodies both the paternal and maternal roles—for Giovanni's son, there is an equally important mother—his role seems fairly traditional. Not just because caring for a child's body is what it is and there's no escaping that, but because the initiation into life itself doesn't seem to have been otherwise problematized. The figure of the psychoanalyst—perpetually present as a wise and compensatory personal guru—guarantees an educational method that should work in any case. The child must never lack attention, but neither firmness. It's necessary not to repress nor to let go completely. Inner nourishment matters as much as inner weaning. One must be mindful of those nearby, never forgetting their fragility. It's hard to escape the impression that this psychoanalysis is, more than a deep dive into the abysses of the self, a system of intelligent shock absorbers.

On this, Brett seems to harbor more doubts than Giovanni. Brett's book gives us everything about him, but not so much about Giovanni. The fact remains that, in the end, Brett wonders whether that experience of love and death could—or should—have been imposed upon/offered to little Zach. In any case, he renders it lighter for his son with some comforting fairy tales.

The relationship between Giovanni and [his son] Stefano, however, is more complicated. Stefano is already a boy, and like boys, he defends himself by withdrawing. When Giovanni decides to tell him that he is sick and that they will lose each other, he wishes equally strongly that Stefano will not suffer and that he will throw himself desperately into his arms. But Stefano stays silent, as if he hasn't fully understood. The measure of their mutual pain is their inability to talk to each other. For Giovanni, it will be a reconfirmation of solitude, something he will struggle to process.

On the other hand, how do you manage death? Not just for your own child, but for yourself, for the person you love, or for others? There is no rationalization possible. The "wonderful" psychoanalyst advises Brett to create distance. What else can the humbler neighbor suggest? Someone will always reassure you that the other person needs you to live. Exactly. And that there's nothing else to say. For Brett, the loss is irreparable. It's a catastrophe of the self, as losses are. Ruthless, Brett—who never grants himself "the beautiful role"—confesses the unbearable nature of Giovanni's agony, his need for that hopeless suffering to end for both of them. But when it finally does end, Brett finds himself halved. The climb out of the abyss begins but perhaps never fully completes. He follows Giovanni to Rome and stays there even after Giovanni is gone, as if staying close to Giovanni's family and the colors of his city meant remaining within his luminous trail.

And then, for both of them, there's also the other family, the one not chosen. For Brett, his was a frustration: not dramatized, but frustration. Since childhood. When he had to explain his situation with Giovanni to his parents, they didn't say, "Son, how can we help you?" but rather something like, "Son, why did you get yourself into this mess?" He expected it, but anticipating such pain doesn't ease it. Giovanni's family was different: a large, cultured, dramatic, and formative family. In the background was the tragic figure of his mother, from whom he always felt he received too little, and in the foreground were his sisters: at first, Flam, his "golden and leaden sister," his first assumption of responsibility, and in the end Manu, the wise one, guided by Eastern philosophies, who was with him in his final months alongside Brett. But the very last moments were for his parents, symbolically or by chance, since people usually die of AIDS without their parents present.

Returning to his blood family, the one he had left when he departed for New York, was perhaps Giovanni's way of returning to his origins as the future slipped away from him. For Brett, it might have been an effort to draw closer to a blood family less lacking than his own. So, do blood and tradition matter? How much do they matter? When do they? At the beautiful tree-lined corner of the Jewish cemetery at Verano where the Rosselli family tomb lies, Giovanni was accompanied by those who had always been part of his life: his mother, his sisters, Stefano, and Stefano's mother, many of us who had crossed paths with him, a few from his early New York years, and, of course, Brett holding Zach in his arms. But he was also accompanied by the rituals of his religion. What had Judaism come to mean for him and for Brett, beyond a golden thread stretching back millennia? From Giovanni's letters, as well as from what we knew of him, there emerges a critical, restless spirit, fundamentally irreligious. At his tomb, a mutual friend recalled King David dancing. Perhaps she was right. Perhaps he, too, had undertaken this exploration of his roots. The Giovanni I remember resembles a modern Peer Gynt more than a young king rejoicing before his God. The prayers ultimately enveloped him in sleep among many others, no longer alone, nestled within a definitive history.

But perhaps, this, too, was something more. In many who were younger than me, and less tethered by memory than I, there was a reborn need for a sense of belonging—not chosen, but acquired at birth—a desire to anchor identity in the paternal genealogy, from which a faith revealed is the most stringent and reassuring manifestation. For many young Jews, it was both a need and a debt. Rediscovering the Law also meant rediscovering exile—a centuries-long negation to be embraced rather than drowned in cosmopolitanism.

This, too, is a sign of our times. Perhaps other writings of Giovanni will tell us more. But I'm not sure if everything must be unearthed, if the end should not also be silence, if compassion does not point to a threshold that cannot be crossed, neither in life nor in death, without violating something. If anything more can be added to Giovanni's biography, nothing will render his time and the way he so determinedly wrote himself into it as vividly as these pages by Brett Shapiro.

These are pages of rare and restrained writing. Brett does not indulge in the ambiguous allure of contemplating pain. From emotions to gestures, from the perception of anguish to that of beginnings—the onset of illness still tentative, its invasion, its darkness, the medicines (what medicines!), the home (what a home!), the clinics (what clinics!), the American and Italian doctors, and the phantom of the Swiss miracle, up to the escape from agony, even from those who love you—everything is told, nothing is shouted. Brett Shapiro may have found consolation in composing the unspeakable into words: "The perception of the object entails the loss of the object," he wrote, and also in processing grief. Certainly, what came out is not just a document but a work capable of existing for itself, of not dissolving with the immediacy that produced it.

When the image of Giovanni dies with those of us who knew him, when AIDS may have been defeated, when times will turn toward other horizons, and those who come after will have their eyes fixed elsewhere, the intelligence of this love and pain will live on in those who take this book into their hands without knowing anything about us.

Rome, July 1993

Dedicated to Stefano and Zachary, our continuum

Defenceless under the night
Our world in stupor lies;
Yet, dotted everywhere,
Ironic points of light
Flash out wherever the Just
Exchange their messages:
May I, composed like them
of Eros and of dust,
Beleaguered by the same
Negation and despair,
Show an affirming flame.

—W. H. Auden, September 1939

1

Anguilla (British West Indies)
Thursday, January 18, 1990

Dearest Flaminia, sister of gold and plum,
    Brisk mornings, hot windless afternoons, long swims in the sea (I've not yet reached the coral reef that protects the bay), lazy afternoons sipping drinks at the side of the pool, long naps, three meals a day. I am reading Saul Bellow, Marguerite Yourcenar, and Fabrizia Ramondino at the same time. I'm making up a bit for a long period of intellectual sloth in which I didn't read anything of value except magazines and newspapers and didn't go to the theatre, concerts, opera, movies. I am plagued by a sense of guilt because with a certain regularity at the gym, I only manage to sustain my impulse to satisfy my sexual appetite. I am truly a sex addict. [...]It's not only down-and-dirty sex that I am used to but also a sense of cosmic fusion with the other that succeeds in inspiring young pretty strangers who need advice and spiritual guidance to call me afterward to see me again (they sometimes succeed), even if I made it clear from the beginning that I am involved in a relationship and am, therefore, not available. I don't kid myself. I know

that I am taking away something from James, even if it is something that he probably can't give me—even if here, with the hot weather, he has become sexually cocky, and we did it TWO TIMES IN ONE DAY (almost a record!). But it is like a slow hemorrhage. Maybe this is one of the reasons that I do it, because I can't stand the idea of belonging completely to one person.

Write back XXXXX! A big big big hug. Gio.

Summer nights in Brooklyn. Stoops and streets choked with people rehydrating—beers, primarily, their discarded receptacles forming by daybreak small cupolas on street curbs and abandoned lots; other, more exotic refreshments, like shaved ice doused in vivid-colored sugar water, or thick rods of sugar cane, adult pacifiers; and for the truly angry or despairing, cheap whisky cloaked in brown paper bags. Clusters of men and women converging around a card table, a ghetto blaster, a crack vial while the stray children find paradise crouched under an open fire hydrant. No one adult is alone, yet all seem unhappy, driven to seek—or is it to forget about—pleasure in the way they are driven outdoors to scramble for the ripple of unstale air. Night after night, I watch this refrain from my own stoop, my one-year-old adopted son Zach crawling on the gated-in segment of concrete, our acreage, exploring the rough mortar and occasional bold weed between the gray slabs, fingering a discarded bottle cap or popsicle stick or simply looking at me with an adoration whose innocence makes me shudder. Miracles occur: I am a father. A virgin birth, a parthenogenetic event—from one man comes this child. Impassable barriers have disappeared. What I want was forbidden, taboo. What was never to be is. The child is real. Yet looking out, so is the adult solitude in immense and boisterous numbers, coated in sweat, all reaching. There must be a way out, or at least a way in. Some adult must be able to be reached.

New York, May 10, 1990

Dearest sister of gold and plum,

It is a rainy Thursday in May. I am at home listening to classical music. The first part of your letter was all about Mamma and the work you are doing in therapy to remove some of the emotional blocks that you use as defense mechanisms in order not to suffer. In your eyes—and maybe objectively as well—I was the favorite child. Yes, it's true, I lived with her, but I always felt that I was on trial, that her acceptance of me was conditional: if I behaved well, was not a nuisance but a good and nice boy, I could stay, otherwise I would be sent back to Babbo. In reality, I too had the feeling of having to forever win her over, that my place with her was never guaranteed.

And, unfortunately, the scars that remain from all this have not healed and still have behavioral consequences. I did IT again. Once again, I behaved sadistically toward someone close to me at a time when he needed my help. It seems that my sense of commitment and responsibility stops at the family threshold: I would say that I was really close when you needed it, and certainly with (my son) Stefano. But with girlfriends and boyfriends, it is a real disaster. There is a little devil that springs up in me and makes me do the most horrible things during a time of need (other people's). The dress rehearsal was a couple of months ago. James had serious back problems and had to stay at home on his back for several days: aside from the pain, there were also practical problems. I literally escaped. I went to East Hampton with Stefano and didn't even call him for two days. We went to Martha together for several sessions and he complained bitterly that I am afraid of his vulnerabilities and flee, and he realized that he can't truly count on me (and isn't this the essence of being together?). But by this time, my flight had already begun. I couldn't take him anymore. He was heavy, and I didn't want to continue with the lies I was fabricating to avoid telling him about my sexual escapades, which would have made him suffer too much (he has very traditional values and believes in monogamy; at this point, we have virtually no sexual relationship, so how can he possibly think that this would be acceptable to me?). For the first time, I had met someone (his name is Marc) with whom there was instantly something more than pure sex. A strong attraction but also the sensation of an emotional flow, very special (in effect, this is the reason for preferring monogamy since things can develop during sexual escapades).

On Sunday morning, while James was sleeping, I left, leaving him a little note that said I needed to be alone and that I would come back that evening for his friend's birthday party. I swear that I had no intention of calling Marc, but I did nevertheless, and spent Sunday with him, reaching new levels of awareness and intimacy. That night, after the party, when James asked me point blank, I couldn't lie. Since then, things have been disastrous. He can't accept that I can be with him and also be having an affair. For the first time, he said that he could accept my having "one or two fucks." Six months ago, that would have been enough, but now I don't want to lie anymore. With Marc, I want to explore the possibility of a fuller relationship. James doesn't accept this, just as he doesn't accept the idea of salvaging the essence of our relationship, that is, affection, friendship, and mutual support, letting sex go, since at this point, it is almost nonexistent anyway. In a heavy (therapy) session with Martha, in which he was extremely angry and cold, he said that if I leave him now, he doesn't want to remain my friend. A bit heavy, huh? Sam is very critical of what I did, and even Martha said that monogamy is a smoke screen and that my real problem is running away when someone needs me.

[...]It's true that one can always be a better person, but maybe we should also look to deepen and accept and appreciate who we are. A big hug, Gio.

2

Giovanni responded to a personal advertisement I had placed in the *Village Voice* at the suggestion of my therapist. During the first year of my son's life, I came to understand how profoundly I needed to be a father: all my lovers had been children. Six months before I put myself on the market for friendship, I had separated from my partner of four and one-half years, Walnes Remy. Walnes, my final adult child, had been sent to his own room, wherever that was, and I wanted an adult partner. Zach and I were living on the first two floors of a charming Tudor-style house I owned in an unsavory neighborhood of Brooklyn, worlds away from the social and cultural amenities of Manhattan where I had lived for six years. I could not lure my friends away from their cosmopolitan enclaves to venture over the Brooklyn Bridge, nor could I find the energy to make the return odyssey once I came home from work and tended to my son. In short, I was stranded and lonely and wanted a bit of company. On another stratum, however, the one where incredulity swells, crests, and breaks, I was dreaming of adventure: when Zach is two or three or so, full of American inoculations and packed with those years of elemental nutrients and calories, father and son, and perhaps a partner, will do something Brett-wild: join the Peace Corps or climb the Himalayas together or at least live abroad. A father and his lover and his kid, not the nuclear family but a familial team, a cemented unit.

Originally, I balked at the idea of placing an ad, feeling I would be thrust into the category of people who held a secret reservoir of unlovability that spawned such an act of self-promotion. However, my therapist convinced me that by placing the ad myself, I'd have control, a situational frame of mind that she traditionally tried to wean me from. She was convinced that this exception was justified.

The ad read: "Gay male, 34, writerly, warm and wise, thinly disguised as corporate executive by day, politically active off hours, single father of an adorable one-year-old, seeks man of similar outlook for friendship plus. Can you change a diaper?" For my sixty-four dollars, I received eighty responses, and Giovanni's was one of eighteen that I decided warranted a telephone follow-up. His letter was a late arrival, and I read it rather cursorily, my original enthusiasm and secret hope for the stars having waned by the forty-fifth letter whose promise of the stars contained a subtext of desperation. "I am nothing and ready to be molded into anything that will make you happy."

Wednesday, May 23, 1990.

Dear VMV6837,

Sure, I can change a diaper! Actually, this is what I did for the best part of the years 1979 and 1980. And playing, going to the playground, to the park, cooking, cuddling, washing, etc. My son, Stefano, was born December 2, 1978, and ever since he has been the emotional centerpiece of my life.

I moved to New York from Rome (Italy) in 1986 for my job: hard times at the beginning, better times later. However, I find the New York gay community quite unresponsive to parenthood. In theory, yes: how cute! In practice, don't bother us (recently, I met a single mother who told me it's exactly the same in the straight community; so maybe it's not gays, it's New York). There are exceptions though. Most notably my best friend, Sam, who over the years has built a real, one-on-one friendship with Stefano. The two have a terrific time together, the kind of rough horseplay and give-and-take that is somehow unreachable for me as the father. And in 1986, I went to a few meetings of the Gay Fathers Group. I liked some of the people very much, but maybe because I was hard-pressed for time or something didn't click, I stopped going after a while.

This summer, Stefano is moving back to Italy where he'll live with his mother. It's something he has wanted to do for a long time, and I couldn't possibly oppose. But I'm going to miss him an awful lot.

Last week, I was scanning compulsively the Personals (like I do with the Obituaries in the *Times*) when I happened onto your ad. I liked it. Not just the part about the kid but I have to say that was what prompted me to write. I wouldn't mind befriending a gay father for whom parenting is obviously essential, and I would like very much to have a small child in my life again. I don't know how possible it is to find romance in the Personals—but friendship certainly! And you yourself in your ad said you're looking for 'friendship plus' (meaning, I suppose, that friendship would do, and anything more is not necessary but wouldn't be rejected—Right?).

Something quickly about me. I'm 36. I had a very intense life and it shows. Some find me handsome, although I'm no California surfer, no preppy, no bodybuilder. In fact, I think I look rather like a disheveled

Central European rabbi! I used to be very radical and gay-lib, now I'm more confused. Besides, as you might have found out for yourself, having the responsibility of a child really changes your outlook on life. Suddenly, having the refrigerator stocked doesn't seem such a despicable goal anymore, nor having an apartment that doesn't look like a tent in a summer camp. I'm still very interested in politics and activism but more as a spectator than a protagonist, also because of my work (I'm the correspondent for an Italian magazine) and the fact that I'm not an American citizen.

Your story seems very interesting. How come you're a single parent? Is it the product of a broken marriage? Or a deliberate choice? I'd like to know, and to tell you my story. Write or call Giovanni Forti 95 Horatio Street Apt. 512 New York 10014 (212) 727-3916.

His handwriting was childlike and unselfconscious, the letter itself refreshingly uncomposed. I called Giovanni several days after receiving his letter and accepted his suggestion that he come to Brooklyn to meet me the following day, Sunday, June 3, 1990.

Up until that point in my selection process, all first—and usually last—dates took place during the work week, during the lunch hour, and near my place of employment. I wanted strict temporal and geographic boundaries to the initial encounters so that I wouldn't have to be preoccupied with how to extricate myself in the event they were a bust. However, something about our conversation, and Giovanni's suggestion, was so lacking in artifice that I was persuaded to consent to an open-ended meeting.

The doorbell rang at the appointed time, and I peered out the diamond-shaped window implanted in my metal fireproof front door to find a short, small-framed, unprimped man with whom, in a matter of hours, and despite my usual resistance, I would fall in love. Zach was in midafternoon nap when Giovanni arrived, and we had the opportunity to spend two hours sitting on the living room rug piecing the preliminary stitches of each other together before Zach's crying activated the baby monitor. Then, the three of us went outside to my small yard where we lay in the grass playing with Zach and continuing the surprisingly easeful ritual of the first date. Giovanni was delighted with Zach and didn't manufacture that overebullience with children that peters out after five minutes, nor the awkwardness I'd observed in so many of my friends who don't have children. He was steady, self-assured, and immensely affectionate. Zach warmed quickly to Giovanni, particularly when he played the Italian version of "This little piggy goes to market" on Zach's toes.

Giovanni and I managed to see each other almost every day until the following weekend. On Monday night I went to his apartment in the Village for dinner and met his eleven-year-old son, Stefano, who treated me to a violin recital after the requisite pasta dinner. The next three afternoons, we had lunch together in the cafeteria of the Time Warner Building where I was working. Giovanni worked only three blocks away. We both had separate plans for the weekend. Zach and I were going to the country with a gay couple who lived in Kew Gardens and also had a one-year-old, and Giovanni was off to Louisiana to interview David Dukes for an article he was writing for *L'Espresso*. That Friday, he helped me drag all the baby accessories, including an unboxed and cumbersome car seat, on the subway to the home of my friends. When we arrived in Kew Gardens, we sat on the sofa and Giovanni took my hand. This was our first physical contact, with the exception of an "accidental" brushing of toes when we were lying barefoot in my yard on the Sunday of our meeting.

On the Sunday evening of our returns, Giovanni called me

to ask me to lunch the following afternoon. He said that he wanted to talk to me about something. Even though only one week had gone by since we met, I couldn't help but wonder, childishly, whether he was going to proffer some declaration of his affections. I suppose, given the courage it required for him to choose to tell me what could have been left untold, at least for a while, it was a declaration of sorts. He confided that he was HIV positive. I felt a lovely taut string snap inside, and my eyes blurred with tears. "Even though I am asymptomatic and have been for four years, I felt you have a right to know." As I later discovered, Giovanni's notion of "asymptomatic" meant anything less than having Karposi Sarcoma or pneumocystis. In April 1989, more than one year before we met, he had written to his father that he "recently had some health problems. Acute anemia forced me to undergo a transfusion that has brought everything almost back to normal. But in the meantime, it was decided that I should suspend AZT. I haven't yet started up again and this makes me a little nervous. Anyway, apart from diarrhea and chronic fatigue, I continue to thank God that I don't have symptoms." And on June 1, 1990, only two days before we had met, he wrote the following letter to his father:

Dearest Babbo,

I am responding to your letter of May 9, which took forever to get here. Since then, we have spoken on the phone unusually frequently because I called (perhaps a little irresponsibly) in moments of physical pain and fear, which I think has only provoked a lot of worrying. In reality, it is useless and wrong, because you are not here, and the phone is too expensive. Therefore, in the future, I will refrain from making these calls, even if I promise to tell you everything that is happening.

This prolonged physical crisis has had its consequences. Above all, it can be seen on my face. I have lost weight, am pale and worn-out looking, and my eye sockets are deep. I am very weak and to go to work for half a day and to come home exhausts me to the point that I sleep two hours in the afternoon and then still go to bed early. I'm no longer a boy and it takes time to recuperate. As far as the psychological consequences, I don't know. In my long sleepless nights, I realize that I am not as strong in fighting the pain and anxiety as I'd thought, and therefore I vacillate in my determination to do everything, in every circumstance, to keep alive. The thought of death has become less abstract, and I have even understood that in certain moments and extreme circumstances, it can seem almost desirable, if only as a form of rest.

When Giovanni told me he was HIV positive, he was straightforward but somewhat ashamed and very nervous about what my reaction might be. "What do you expect me to say?" I asked. "That I never want to see you again?" "I hope not," he replied. "Of course not. That's ridiculous. You are not a virus. You have a virus. I like you. I want to continue seeing you, being with you." We both started to cry. "Oh, thank God," he said. "I was so terrified that you would decide not to see me again." I took his hand and smiled into his eyes. Our first tears, only one week after we'd met.

For about six months before his death, I sometimes wished that I had decided not to see him again after that Monday lunch. I might still have been suffering from my circumstantial isolation, but I wondered if that condition would have been preferable to the one I was finding myself in. That wish, fantasy, torment, escape had nothing to do with love. I loved Giovanni. But with each passing day, he did become more and more his virus. And with each passing day grew my futile possessiveness, my desire to reclaim him, to wrench him loose from both the illness and the social and familial matrix in which he was embedded and to extend into a lifetime those few symptom-free months we had. The syndrome was the third party, the anti-partner, in our relationship, vying for him with a power against which I was unable to compete. And in the end, of course, as we both knew but never dared believe completely, it would win.

3

The week of Giovanni's confession we had lunch together every day and spoke on the phone in the evenings. Since we both had children to come home to after work, the terrain of the mattress remained unexplored for a short while. It was comforting to know that our demanding jobs and our families assured—or so we thought—that we didn't rush headlong into the recumbent relationship. There was no evidence of the virus. The diarrhea and chronic fatigue that Giovanni had written about a year earlier, and which became a daily part of our life a few months later, were not visible to me at that time. I don't know whether they were actually in remission or whether Giovanni managed to control these "nonsymptoms" when we were together. He was highly energetic, 125 pounds, muscular. It was easy not to think or talk about the presence of the virus or its inevitable progress. The only reminder was "Beedie," Zach's word for Giovanni's cream-colored plastic pill box which was set to beep every four hours to remind him to take his AZT, Bactrim, Xovirax, and other assorted medications that would vary as time went on and, eventually, increased to a quantity which Beedie was no longer large enough to store. At that point, Beedie was used as our alarm clock. Its beep is not jarring and nudges one to wakefulness.

Giovanni and Stefano spent the following weekend at my house. They slept together on the sofa bed in the living room. When Stefano had fallen asleep, Giovanni crept into my bedroom, as planned, and we made love until four in the morning. Zach woke up at 6:30, his usual hour, and Giovanni rose to the occasion with an energy and enthusiasm that I was able to take for granted. Subsequently, Giovanni and Stefano spent many evenings at my house, arriving at my door with shoestring licorice for Zach and a change of clothes for Giovanni for work. We'd get through the day on a few hours of sleep, our eyes burning like semaphores into the previous night's expedition. We'd depart for work together in the morning, overlapping hands around the subway pole, and holding up our newspapers with our free hand. It was our honeymoon period, always kept anchored by diapers to be changed, bottles to be warmed, homework to be done, hot meals—often barbecues—to be prepared.

Stefano graduated from elementary school at the end of June and flew back to Italy to live with his mother, Giovanna Pajetta, who had returned to Italy in May. The month of July was spent intensively developing the three-way relationship between Giovanni, Zach, and me. It was soon clear that we were to be a family, and Giovanni and I decided that we would live together when he returned on Labor Day weekend from his one-month vacation in Vermont.

New York, June 4, 1990

Dear Mamma,

Just a brief greeting and a hug. I had a long bout with my teeth: first my wisdom teeth, then a bacterial infection in my throat, and this morning a root canal and a filling in another tooth on the left side that chose this moment to crumble, revealing a dreadful cavity below. All of this at a time when, as you know, Stefano is staying with me because Giovanna returned to Italy (although right now she is in Washington following the Bush-Gorbachev summit). To top it off, my relationship with James is exploding: I asked that we change it into an "open relationship," and he refused outright. We had a few stormy sessions with my therapist, Martha. We haven't seen each other for several weeks now (also because I was always at home with Stefano and James had no desire to come), but tomorrow night we are going out to dinner.

Anyway, in spite of everything I've just said, I am in a pretty good mood. I am always more decisive about taking advantage of my increasing free time to write fiction, and I have many ideas in my head. I'm looking forward to the vacation in August with Sam, Stefano, Emanuela, and Rita in Vermont—and in the longer run—my return to Italy. It occurred to me that I can request a mortgage at Casagit and we could, therefore, buy two apartments, a little bigger and a little prettier (who knows, maybe we could even throw a small terrace into the bargain) from the profits of the sale of your via Luciani apartment. What do you think? Have you started looking into it, talking to a few agencies, as we spoke about during Easter at Cenci? I have a good recollection of that day and I hope that in moments of despair you are able to realize that even during depression one can have good moments—it is not a permanent state. You've had them before and you'll have them again.

Stefano is growing at a dizzying rate. He has a few hairs under his armpits and maybe pubic hair as well, but he is modest and won't let me see, wrapping himself in his bathrobe immediately after his bath. He is extremely sarcastic and critical and very witty too. His latest obsession is buying little medieval soldiers and dragons à la *Lord of the Rings* and painting them with fine-haired paintbrushes. His room is in complete chaos and always looks like a bomb hit. He doesn't give hugs or kisses, not even before going to bed or when he leaves for school. In short, the perfect pre-adolescent! I admit that at times it's a little difficult for me to "let go," and not a few people say that maybe not only bad comes from bad, and the temporary and relative separation from Stefano could even have positive effects.

My best, a big hug—Gio.

Giovanni and I spent one evening in early July strolling along the Hudson River, across the street from his apartment in the Village. He told me that he was planning to stop therapy after ten years. He then opened his wallet, took out a membership card to a bathhouse, and ripped it up. "The photograph you gave me of Zach and you replaces this," he said. The ensuing conversation revealed that Giovanni frequented the baths on an average of three times a week, and he had done so for years, even through all of his various and numerous relationships. This bit of history deeply disturbed me, particularly since its abrupt symbolic ending didn't have any discernible evolution or concrete motive other than the general one of his love for me. Moreover, I couldn't help but think, unfairly, that it was this very promiscuity that had gotten him infected in the first place. I didn't like feeling responsible for his commitment to fidelity. For just as mysteriously as I had supposedly inspired it, it could just as mysteriously be broken through some deficiency or mistake I might make in the future. The well-intended gesture, and the history it tried to banish, made me extremely uncomfortable as well as insecure. Only months later, the issue of fidelity would be "resolved," when Giovanni's sexual appetite and ability to perform would be eradicated by the virus.

...

The long July 4th weekend was spent with friends in East Hampton. It was a glorious four days, marred only by one incident. Giovanni had recently separated from James Revson, his boyfriend of two and one-half years. James happened to be at his country home in East Hampton for the holiday weekend, and Giovanni decided to visit him in order to tell him that he'd met me. Unfortunately, the conversation turned acrid, with James asking Giovanni to leave and insisting that he never speak to him again. Out of respect for James's wish, Giovanni never did; nor did he attend the funeral when James died of AIDS about one year later.

I had a similar unpleasant encounter when we returned from East Hampton. After separating from Walnes, I had encouraged him to maintain his relationship with Zach since we were together at the time I adopted Zach when he was three days old. More and more frequently when Walnes came to visit Zach, he would find my "friend" Giovanni at the house. On one such occasion, after we'd returned from East Hampton, Giovanni and I had gone for a walk, leaving Walnes and Zach at the house. On our return, Walnes pulled me aside to inform me that Giovanni was HIV positive. He claimed that he had seen Giovanni at his clinic (Walnes had been diagnosed HIV positive about five months before). As it turned out, Giovanni had never been to the clinic. Rather, Walnes had rifled through my closet during our absence and found Giovanni's overnight bag which contained Giovanni's medications, the names of which were all too familiar to Walnes. Poor Walnes was hoping that I would stop seeing Giovanni once his scarlet letter was revealed, as he was convinced that that was the reason I had asked him to move out of the house. When I told Walnes that I had known about Giovanni's condition since we first met, he began sobbing and left the house. I saw a healthy Walnes for the last time one week later when he came to Zach's two-year birthday party. He arrived well ahead of the party to deliver the cake, spent most of his one-hour visit talking with my mother in the kitchen, and departed before the party began. The next time I saw him, in May 1991, he was eighty-four pounds, unable to move, and barely able to speak. Walnes died on July 29, 1991, only a few weeks after James died. His funeral was held on the first day of the one-month vacation that Giovanni, Stefano, Zach, and I had on Fire Island, during which time Giovanni's already deteriorating condition was becoming critical. By the end of our vacation, he himself weighed ninety-four pounds.

4

Bread Loaf (Vermont), August 13, 1990, 4:40 pm

Dearest Mother,

Here I am with the promised letter. It seems such a long, long time since I've had a really quiet moment, and I dedicate it to you. I just woke up from an afternoon nap. Silence. The house is simple, not especially old, made of wood, with many skylights, and it is virtually one single space with no private enclosed rooms. Only with this special group of people could I feel comfortable enough to come here to stay. It is furnished haphazardly—rural New England (you know the style) — and is at the end of a dirt road in the middle of the woods, so no one passes by.

I think that we'll be able to have an enjoyable and relaxing vacation, even if Stefano frets a bit. Without kids his age, it is difficult to keep him entertained, and he doesn't take long walks alone or read for hours as I did at his age. We have *Gulliver's Travels* in the unabridged original, but he refuses to read it with the lame excuse that he already knows the story. But for the next few days, we have planned a series of activities and excursions, and Sam and Emanuela have a special rapport with him which takes some of the pressure off me.

Rita made a comment today at lunch that shocked me. She said that she had never even tried to read David Leavitt because she knows that his subject matter is about human relationships, and writers who are preoccupied with this subject annoy her, like Thomas Mann (!). Then it came out that she never read Jane Austen or George Eliot. Hmm. Hopefully, I'll get to know her better as days go by and will discover that she has a fine soul. Another thing that happened at lunch is that I began to see an alliance between Manu and Sam that is slightly against me: they both said that what they value most in people is sincerity and genuineness and they were outraged that I value intelligence more. A bit of a disagreement is more than healthy as long as it doesn't turn into a Holy Alliance (Holy in all senses of the term!).

Before leaving for Vermont, Stefano and I went to dinner at S. G.'s where there was the usual colony of chirping Italian journalists. I drank a little too much, was judgmental, pompous, apodictical. I hated myself and once again remembered why I normally avoid such gatherings (the worst comes out in me).

Then, the last evening with Brett and Zach, the last night with Brett. My heart is a little broken. When I return from Vermont, everything will be different because Brett and Zach will be moving in with me. I want this very much but I also have a very warm spot for his little house in Brooklyn with the backyard where we spent two enchanting months.

Two problems: my crisis of abstinence without a telephone, TV, or newspapers (I promised Stefano that I won't run around like a wild man looking for them, and I didn't read any papers yesterday or today!!!!) and a sense of guilt about *L'Espresso*, what with the Mideast crisis (their fault, not thinking to fill in for me—but); and, above all, the need to tell Stefano that Brett and Zach are moving in with me. I'm afraid he'll be jealous of the little one, and that he won't express his feelings. I must choose the right words. Relief over the presence of Manu and Sam. But this is tomorrow's task! A great big kiss—Gio 6:25 p.m.

Bread Loaf (Vermont), August 20, 1990

Dearest Babbo,

I am responding relaxedly to your letter of August 4 because I can give it to Emanuela to give to you. I still have ten days before she leaves, so I can write to you at length and without any hurry. Even if it is in fits and starts because, I don't know why, we're always in a race, even in this kind of setting, in the thick of the Vermont woods without a telephone or television. Right now, for example, I am writing to you just as the gang is getting ready to leave to join some of Sam's friends for a barbecue (we are bringing the chicken and the charcoal). We should have already left, and the fact that we haven't is because the girls, Emanuela and Rita, have chosen this very moment to make the bed, to take all the things they think they will need, to freshen up, and God only knows what else women come up with to make themselves late. I am in the loft where I sleep with Stefano and I can see him below. He is playing around with his compact video game and Sam is reading something. Both of them have been ready for some time. The late afternoon sunlight and the shade from the leaves penetrate all the windows and skylights in the cool and dark wood house and play on my table. Even if the external circumstances of our life in these days are of great quiet and immersion in nature, my restlessness has hardly slackened, let alone stopped. Anyway, it has nothing in common with the Russians: I am reading *The Idiot* and nobody does anything but scream, shout, insult, ask forgiveness, kiss each other's hands, start vendettas, have mystical crises, interrupt oneself, have a philosophical discussion, scream and shout and insult and interrupt oneself in turn [...]

August 21. A draggy afternoon, after having slept eleven hours (from 11 at night until 10 in the morning). I told Sam that everyone in this house would have an autumn of transition and change and transformation, him included. [...]I am more joyous and excited than afraid of the transformation that awaits me this autumn, even if there are always underground currents of anxiety. My life is about to undergo an enormous change, not sought out or foreseen, but one that instantly seemed so obvious and natural that I would have to be blind not to do it, even if it may seem, in the eyes of good sense, blind to do it.

I am starting up a family again. On September 1, Brett Shapiro (his last name is the "Smith" of the Jews, or the "Rossi" if you prefer) and his son Zach are moving in with me, and it has already been agreed upon that at the end of 1991, when I intend to return to Rome, they will come with me and live with me and Stefano. I think that you will be surprised. I don't think I've mentioned Brett to you until now. After all, there hasn't been much time. I met him only on June 4 and I don't think that in this period I wrote to you; furthermore, in the beginning of a relationship, one tends not to talk about it for fear that it will be spoiled. But now there are announcements to make...

Brett is 35 years old, from Philadelphia, balding, with dirty-blond hair, short (but quite a bit taller than me, which doesn't take much). He is very sweet, full of love, and very giving. A little more than two years ago, he legally adopted a newborn whose name is Zachary, and he is completely dedicated to him. He works as a personnel director in a big office in New York on the thirty-ninth floor of the Time Life Building on Fiftieth Street (on which, a few blocks to the east, is the Newsweek building, on the thirty-sixth floor of which is my office—funny coincidence and also useful). But he does this work only for the money; his real vocation is writing very beautiful stories, none of which have been published yet, and a lot of travel articles and articles on issues of Judaism. He lives in a little house in Brooklyn with a small backyard, in a neighborhood almost completely inhabited by Caribbeans and West Indians with their sing-song accents, their habit of hanging out on the sidewalks chatting until late at night, the old ones seated on chairs, pungent odors of goat meat emanating from the windows.

I am reluctant to talk about my feelings for Brett and Zach. Too many times in the past I flaunted, defined, labeled. Let the facts speak for themselves. I will say that I am very happy and aware. Stefano also said he is happy and added that they are nice (this I know for certain is true). Whether he might become jealous in the future because he'll be far away and there will be another child in his room, I don't know, or vice versa, as Manu went through, worried about leaving me alone and it being a relief for him to leave me in company. (One could therefore fear that he is one of those that Alice Miller talks about in *The Drama of the Gifted Child*: completely attuned to the needs of the parents and not his own—but I don't think this is the case.) Speaking about transformations, Stefano is changing in a striking way. His feet are now a great deal bigger than mine, and he is much stronger. His voice is going through the change, with those uncontrollable squeaks, and a pungent smell comes from him which he isn't aware of or he finds pleasing because he never wants to wash and it's always a fight. He has hair under his armpits, and I imagine even pubic hair, but I don't know because I haven't seen him naked in many months. Even here, where we sleep together, his newfound modesty makes him go through incredible contortions to avoid being seen naked. He is basically happy, and if he has occasional bad moods, he doesn't cling to them stubbornly. He has individual and special relationships with each of the adults here, very pleasant; more complex with me, sustained by sarcasm, criticism, refusal, need.

I realize that I haven't responded at all to the main theme of your letter, which was death, but I don't feel at all in a condition to do so: the fact that I wrote about it in *L'Espresso* came from their request, not from my own initiative. But clearly, since I had to do it, I tried to do my best, which included giving it the proper reflection. I hope that your vacation in Spain was a success. Let me know. A big hug. Giovanni.

Bread Loaf, Vermont, Tuesday, August 22

Dear Brett,

I've just finished reading *The Idiot* and I feel the

need to communicate with you. Yesterday I tried to reach you at work and I failed. Today I hope to be luckier. But I want to write to you as well.

The most bizarre episode just happened to me. I was taking a shit in the bathroom, reading John Cheever's "Journals" in the *New Yorker,* and I was standing up wiping myself (at this point of the narration, Sam interrupted: "You stand up to wipe yourself?" a whole debate ensued on the respective advantages of sitting or standing, Stefano was summoned and asked his opinion, and the punch line of the story was partially diluted) when I suddenly noticed a fat woman I had never seen before, standing in front of the window (ground floor) looking ahead and taking notes. For a brief, paranoid moment I thought she was writing about me but I almost immediately realized that she was, in fact, jotting down the numbers of the electricity meter that happens to be next to the bathroom window. Either she hadn't seen me, or more likely, she chose to ignore me. At any rate, she quickly disappeared, and when I went back to the living room bursting with the urgency to tell what had just happened, her orange truck was going off in a trail of dust.

Our little community here is not exactly disintegrating but eroding at the edges, losing coherence. We wake up later and later. The last few mornings, Stefano has been sleeping in, and it was only the two of us, Manu and I, for yoga. Yesterday I didn't feel like doing it at all, but I felt guilty about it. This morning, however, I felt bad and wanted to be bad and announced that I wasn't going to do yoga. But Manu changed my mind, getting me interested with new Kundalini types of exercise (I was getting bored with the old ones). We took our usual late breakfast (we finished at 11:20) with cereal and fruit and toast and coffee and juice. Then I convinced Stefano to wash his armpits and make the bed. The plan of the day was to go to the little airport of Warren and go gliding or at least to get information about it, but Manu had accidentally thrown her camera to the floor and maybe broken it and wanted to go fix it. Now she and Rita have been gone for quite a long time (it's almost 2:00 p.m.). It's not exactly that we don't do anything, because we do, but it's usually late, and our goals are simple and nearby, and it's rare that we manage to be all five, which my shepherd dog's instinct would require. Yesterday, Sam and I went on our bikes to the beavers' pond. He taught me how to pedal in slow motion up a steep hill. At the meadow, Stefano and Manu joined us by car, and I hung my bike on the rack in the back of the car. On our way, walking in the path we saw a chipmunk and two frogs, and at the pond we saw not one but two beavers and a moose! But the beavers didn't slap their flat tails noisily like they had done the other day when Stef and I went to the pond alone.

Right now, I'm sitting at the desk in the loft and I can see down in the living room Sam taking a nap on a banquette. I know that Stefano is out on the screened-in porch reading *Dungeon*, a fantasy book that he bought yesterday during an expedition with Rita to Middlebury. The house is perfectly still. From the skylight in front of me, I can see tree leaves and a slice of sky. Nature is all around, peeping through the many large windows and encompassing the porch. The only noise is the stream singing down the valley and the regular humming of the refrigerator. Stefano turns the pages and sighs from time to time. He just came up here to get some Ritz crackers that I had on the table. A strip of sunlight on the floor.

I miss you so much that my heart aches. I never wanted to need anyone, with the partial exception of Stefano (but, as Manu told me, "children are different"). I probably miss you less than you miss me, if I can judge your feelings correctly from the phone calls, but I still miss you more than I've ever missed any other adult in my life. It scares me but it also fills me with an exquisite delight: so, I'm like the others! I can love and feel the lack of the beloved like everybody else! Besides, soon I'll be in New York and I will be able to hug you, and our new life together will start. We may choose never to part for long but if we hadn't had this August separation, I would have never known something very important about my feelings for you.

Now that I've finished *The Idiot*, I feel satiated but empty at the same time. I don't know what to read next. I have three options: *Barbarians at the Gate*, about the takeover of R. J. Nabisco, *The Four-Gated City*, a fantasy by Doris Lessing, and *The Buddha of Suburbia* by the author of *My Beautiful Laundrette* (coincidentally, the last two are British). I could also give myself some rest, given that Saturday I will probably spend seven or eight hours on a bus or on a train and I'll have plenty of time to read then. I would like to surprise you and show up Saturday night in Chester Court unannounced, but I'm not sure you would appreciate it.

Stefano is totally enthralled by his book and has covered our bed with cracker crumbs. I think I'll go either on the porch or outside in the sun and do absolutely nothing. Not read, not write, just be, and try to calm down this overexcited mind of mine.

Wednesday, August 23. It's 8:30 a.m., which for our household is really early. Everybody is still sleeping but

Sam, who's in the bathroom. Everything is perfectly silent. Last night, I went to bed at 10:30, so when this morning I woke up I decided not to go back to sleep as I usually do. Today at 1:00, we have the appointment to go gliding which means that once more we won't be able to go climbing Mount Abraham. We take turns in worrying that we don't do enough and in reminding the others that "vacation" means, literally, "emptiness."

Mostly we are cheerful, pretty much on the silly side (we have our mottos that we repeat dozens of times a day: "here and now" that becomes "awareness of the hereness and nowness," and "ugly but good"), and we giggle and laugh a lot. Last night after dinner (squash soup, ratatouille and rice, cantaloupe: an orange dinner), we played a game based on drawing segments of the body, folding the sheet of paper so as to leave only two lines, and passing it to the next person to complete. The results were hilarious. Stefano seems in a happy mood, but I wonder if it's the right thing for him to spend a vacation with only adults. On the other hand, I remind myself that all the past years I had organized vacations revolving completely around him, sometimes disregarding my own needs, and I felt it was time for a change. However, this that should have been the perfect Giovanni-size kind of vacation turns out to be less than perfect, chiefly because you're not here. This scares me. Is this the famous "dependence" that everybody is talking about, especially women, trying to learn tricks to escape it? I would like to strike an Olympian balance with intensity of feelings, glowing in the other's presence, but also self-sufficiency and productivity. In a word, harmony. Do you think it's too ambitious a goal to strive for? Do you share it? I don't think you're the "Sturm und Drang" type, who doesn't believe love is for real unless it's accompanied by big scenes, fights, reconciliations, swearings, forgivings, and a torrent of words. Already in this letter, I've been more explicit about my feelings than my custom is. Part of me thinks that feelings are like rare flowers and should be left alone. But I also know better. What I need is a lot of routine, a lot of diaper changing and dishwashing. Interspersed in all this, words of love seem less theatrical and less threatening. In short, I want to live with you. But I WILL be living with you! In a week from now. How utterly strange. When I was writing to my father, I took pains to explain to him how obvious this choice was, almost common-sensical, but now that I'm alone with you, I'm struck with the enormity of it. Will you give me your hand, Mr. Shapiro? Will you take me as your faithful husband, in richness and poverty, in health and in illness, to love you and protect you?

 Now that I know Zach is coming back from Philadelphia Saturday at 4:00, I have decided to surprise you after all and show up unexpectedly Saturday night. How will a "control freak" like you act? See you soon, thank God, Giovanni.

New York, Tuesday, August 28, 1990

Dear Flaminietta,
 A day of total, extreme laziness. Yesterday night, I had a slight fever, so I decided to stay home. Tonight, Emanuela, Stefano, and Rita arrive from Niagara Falls, and Saturday, the day that Manu leaves for Rome, Brett and Zach are moving in. Therefore, in reality,

this is the last occasion for me to stay alone in my apartment while it is still mine alone. What is about to happen is very exciting, and I have been wanting a few hours of solitude to reflect a little on it. But—contrary to what you might think—I am not good at being introspective, so I'll write to you about it; it is a good time to reply to you, knowing that soon you will have these pages in your hand. (I'm giving the letter to Manu who will be in Rome on Sunday.)[...]

I'm starting up a family again. If you are surprised by the speed, you shouldn't be. I have known Brett only since June 4th and I am aware that this might seem impulsive. In reality, it is less impulsive than it seems because I had been preparing for it for a long time, only I hadn't found the right person (James wasn't it, this is certain, but it doesn't mean that he isn't a person full of qualities or that I don't care about him, even if, unfortunately, he isn't speaking to me right now). My desires and feelings crystalized around Brett, and everything that has happened since confirms the soundness of this choice. If at times I have the cold sweats over what is about to happen (and who wouldn't?), it is not about Brett but about the thing in itself. After all, it has been seven years since I have lived with another adult, when I left Manuela Fontana's house to be with Stefano, and I am very used to doing things in my own way. Living together means compromises and criticism and modifications in behavior and habits. [...]Brett was absolutely horrified when he discovered that I don't make the bed every day.

Besides which, I have never lived with a man, and this creates two kinds of problems, internal and external. When you live with a woman, however eccentric or nonconformist you might be, there is always the comfort of the roles (which you can fall back on or draw back from). With another man, everything is unexplored territory. And the world? How will it react? Will it take us as seriously as a heterosexual couple? I trust that Stefano, you, Manu, Mamma and Babbo will, but the rest? Friends? The working world, the other journalists, the administration of *L'Espresso*, the teacher at the school where Zach will go, the bank? I have no desire to nail myself on a cross, but neither do I have the intention to accept anything less than the way people treat any couple who is not married but lives together.

Finally, and perhaps above all, the responsibility that I am taking on with Zach. Children are not very interested in legal issues, particularly at two years, but for all legal intents and purposes, I am becoming Zach's other parent. This is happening even before the move! It is true that I already did this another time, but I was younger and more energetic, and I wasn't HIV positive. Zach is delightful but he is absolutely indefatigable and more physical than I remember Stefano being at the same age. Sometimes at the end of the day, I am completely exhausted, but also happy, and I believe that this is what is important. I was very frightened about Stefano's departure for Italy (the day after tomorrow), and even now I know that I'll miss him terribly, but in some way, I feel more balanced. And I think that even he is content that he's not leaving me alone.

So, what do you think? But it is difficult to render feelings in a letter. Manu can tell you more, at least her impressions. A big hug. Gio.

The one-month separation from Giovanni in August 1990 happened too soon. There was still a fantastical quality to our relationship, a seductive mist we inhabited that kept edges, frontiers and defined surfaces out of reach, giving our passage a sensation of perpetual unity. The mist lifted, like a dream shattered by an alarm clock when Giovanni abruptly left for this remote, telephoneless spot with his sister, Emanuela, and her friend Rita, Sam, and Stefano. I was in the tactile world and felt like a shard of my former self, back in my isolated situation, which was exacerbated by having had a taste of communion as well as a case of Lyme disease that I'd caught apparently during our four-day visit to East Hampton. Keeping up with Zach when I was racked by constant fevers and headaches was a torture, but as the illness had been diagnosed early, it was treated promptly and soon passed. I looked forward to the daily pay-phone calls from Giovanni and his many anecdotes of long hikes and bike rides through the countryside, and of the feasts and yoga sessions coordinated by his sister. I felt deprived sweating it out in Brooklyn with Prospect Park or Coney Island as my only havens; still, our plans for Zach and me to move into Giovanni's apartment on September 1 kept my spirits up, and several times during that month Zach and I spent the afternoon at Giovanni's apartment. Giovanni and I had considered the other cohabitation possibilities: Giovanni moving into my house, our finding a new place together. We opted against finding a new place since we had already discussed the probability that we would move to Rome when Giovanni's contract expired in December 1991 and chose for me to make the move into Giovanni's "space" because of the challenge it would present to my controlling nature.

    I'd always promised myself that I would not enter too swiftly into a relationship, especially so when I became a parent. Nevertheless, we became a united family less than three months after we met. I had no questions or hesitations in my mind about the success or seriousness of our commitment. And I sensed immediately that Giovanni, in inevitable times of conflict, was not capable of resorting to malice. I admired his spirit, his intellect, his curiosity, his vitality. He was my best friend. And I loved him. On another level, however, his illness accelerated all of our decisions. We never knew how little time we would have.

5

Zach spent the night before the move at the "new" apartment with Giovanni so that I could focus exclusively on the physical move. I had occupied myself during the last week of Giovanni's vacation with crating those possessions that I didn't want to take and stacking them neatly in the basement. Since I owned the four-family building in which Zach and I were living, I was planning to rent out our apartment and needed to have it in move-in condition.

The van arrived at Giovanni's at noon. Zach was napping and, miraculously, slept through the entire unloading process. Giovanni was eager to unpack the fifty-four boxes of books, and in the time it took him to put them on the shelves (he spent as much time leafing through the books as he did putting them away), I had completely unpacked and arranged the remaining eighty-five boxes. I recall being somewhat annoyed by his seemingly minor contribution.

The divisions of labor soon fell into place. Judith, Zach's nanny from the time he was eight months old, took care of Zach while we worked. She also did the routine housekeeping and occasionally cooked dinner. The rest of the domestic chores—grocery shopping, making repairs, keeping the house in order, etc.—fell primarily on me since I was less laissez-faire than Giovanni. We enrolled Zach in a very pricey preschool which he went to three mornings a week. Giovanni took him to school and gave him a bath; I put him to bed, and on Sundays,

Giovanni woke up with Zach in order to let me sleep in. I also had one night off a week in order to give Giovanni and Zach time alone together as well as to allow me to refamiliarize myself with Manhattan evenings. Our life revolved around our family and our home. Occasionally, we went to dinner or the theatre with friends, but more often, and quite often, we had friends to the house for dinner or Sunday brunch. We were extremely proud of all that we had, and we wanted so much to share our happiness. Our lovemaking was frequent, ardent, far-reaching, our private joy. We decided that when we moved to Rome, we would make provision in our living quarters for what we called the "white room," a small, unfurnished, unadorned room where we would spend an hour or two several times a week alone without words or gestures, a place to grow through the rarity of stillness, a shared womb.

New York, September 13, 1990

Dear Mammozzi,

How are you? For me, my return from Vermont was partly difficult because I miss Stefano enormously, and partly exciting because Brett and Zach moved in with fifty-four boxes of books, a piano, and two cats. For now, we are on our honeymoon, and I am relishing the domestic bliss that, in a certain sense and in such a comprehensive way, I never had. If only Stefano were here, my happiness would be complete. He gets along with Brett and enjoys playing with Zach. Brett is nurturing, full of love, child oriented. Zach is a little devil of quicksilver, and after a few hours with him, I am exhausted. A kiss, Gio.

Zach's and my relationship was intensive, perhaps too much so, and Giovanni often chose not to take any initiative to wean

Zach away from me. He preferred to develop his relationship with Zach alone without the possibility of my intervention, rather than when the three of us were together, during which time he tended to withdraw, feeling that the competition was daunting. The only times the three of us successfully spent time together was at the Bleecker Street playground, a child's oasis, triangular and verdant, set in the middle of three major thoroughfares in the Village, where we often went on weekends if we had no other plans. Here, Zach was instantly drawn to the other children, and they became his primary audience and playmates. His parent-specific needs were diffused into more generalized ones. If he wanted a leg to hide behind when he was playing tag or a hand to help him climb the jungle gym, any adult limb would do the trick. In this setting, Giovanni and I were able to spend hours observing and playing with him on an equal footing.

Giovanni explained to me that he'd never had to compete simultaneously in a three-way relationship before since Stefano split his time between living with him and living with his mother. It is painful to look back to those inchoate times of adjustment. As difficult as our personality clashes sometimes could be, they were still rough surfaces that could be polished in time. Time, however, was precisely what was to be denied us, taking with it many of the opportunities for negotiating compromise. I am sure that Giovanni would have given anything to eventually have gained Zach's trust to the point where he could put him to bed, or for the three of us to play ball. But within months, Giovanni was asleep long before Zach's bedtime and, shortly after, simply walking to the bathroom required all of his effort.

New York, Monday, September 17, 1990

Dear Mamma,

Just a few lines. I tried to call you two times, on

Friday and again today, but you weren't there. I wanted first of all to thank you for going to Pajetta's funeral. I know how little you like these things, but I think that for Stefano it was important that someone from the other side of the family was there to share his sorrow. Unfortunately, I wasn't by his side. I'd already booked a flight for 9 p.m. Thursday the 21st that would have gotten me to Rome 11 a.m., just in time for the viewing, the state funeral, and the family funeral at Taino. But after speaking with Stefano, I didn't get a sense of his need. [...]In the end, I phoned Giovanna. She cried as soon as she heard my voice, yet she was affectionate and considerate and insisted that there was no need for me to come. Therefore, I canceled the reservation. Then in the following days, I felt torn and confused watching the funeral, seeing Stefano looking very serious on TV (it was shown here on cable), and reading in *Corriere della Sera* that he was extremely emotional. [...]I felt that I should have been there.

Anyway, it's passed and useless to cry over spilled milk. I'm coming to see Stefano at the end of October. I'll be in Rome on the morning of the 26th (don't tell him—it's a surprise—I want to show up when school lets out).

It's been a long time since I've heard from you and much longer since I've received any letters from you. Emanuela gives me news of you but always through her filter. I'd like to know first-hand how you are.

I, aside from funeral tremors and missing Stefano, am very well. I am very focused on my personal life, in gaining Zach's trust, on building a warm and cozy family nest. Brett is perfect. We often have people to dinner, and he cooks very well. Have you read "Roads to Rome," the last short story in David Leavitt's book? Did you grin, recognizing the thinly disguised biographical information of at least five people you know?

Now I really have to start cracking at work. I have a deadline for a piece on Dinkins, and now that I am a family man I can no longer pull an all-nighter.

A big hug, your beloved Gio

> New York, Rosh Hashanah,
> first day of the year 5751
> (or Thursday, September 20, 1990 AD)

Dearest Mamma,

Your letter of September 12 gave me enormous pleasure. [...]It's your first missive in a long time. Even if in the letter you say that you're not doing very well, the fact that you did write at all seems to indicate a new vitality, as well as your use of the key phrase "it's up to me." Not that it is easy, but it's sine qua non. Also, the phone call from the other day and the fact that you went to the Pajetta funeral make me think that you are more attentive to the needs of others and more tuned in to the world, less inward. And for the first time in such a long time, you really want to know how I am. You ask me a lot of questions, which I won't answer with mock jokes like the son of the writer Lalla Romano who receives a letter from his mother containing some twenty questions, and answers like this: 1. yes. 2. no. 3. sometimes. 4. only when it rains. 5. no. 6. yes. And so it went, him knowing, wickedly, that his mother hadn't kept a copy of her questions.

Anyway, let me answer seriously. Yes, I am still going to Martha, once a week. In the first session after the vacation, I announced my intention to stop therapy, and to my slight disappointment, she said she was enthusiastic and convinced that I can go it alone. So, now it is I who am stalling, and each week I bring new fascinating information so that we will never set a date for a final session. But I think that between September and October, we should finish. Help!! I've been in therapy for more than ten years, between Gindro and Martha, and I no longer know how to live without it. However, Martha is, fortunately, not a strict Freudian and I could always go to her for an occasional session if I needed a minor tune-up.

My health is good, even if my T4 cells have dropped, alas, to a record low of 128. (I jokingly say that as long as they remain higher than my weight, which is 125 pounds, there's no need to worry.) I go to the bathroom a lot, sometimes it is loose, and sometimes with extreme urgency. Sometimes I have night sweats. One night, I had a slight fever, but the fact remains that I am the ONLY ONE among my friends and acquaintances (all HIV negative) who has not had the flu or a cold in more than four years. I tire easily and sleep a lot (if left to my own, I can sleep even nine to ten hours). I am taken care of lovingly by Brett, who does everything to prevent Zach from waking me up and cooks me good meals like a real Jewish mother. (I gorge myself but I don't understand why I don't gain a pound.) I continue to go to the gym, if sporadically, and before lifting weights, I always do twenty minutes on the bicycle at a number three level of difficulty (the equivalent of six and one-half miles on a steep incline).

Daily life: currently very domestic, as you can imagine. I wake up between seven and eight. Mondays, Thursdays, and Fridays I take Zach to school. I go to the office, where I have some difficulty concentrating and being productive. Every two or three days, I send a little letter to Stefano with comics clipped out of the newspaper. (Today, his first day of school, I called him, and he said to me: "Don't send me so many letters because they make me feel guilty since I don't write back.") Around 6 or 6:30 I come home. I was able to separate our mealtime from Zach's because Brett was becoming very nervous and annoyed with Zach since he is not a great eater or very disciplined. So, we give him a little meal, then I give him a bath, at 8:30 Brett puts him to bed and we eat afterwards, calmly, something which at first upset Brett, who is used to eating at 6:30 (his parents eat at 5:30!), but now he is used to it. We rarely watch TV, he is teaching me some piano, we read a little, straighten up, I run the dishwasher, and at 10:30 or 11, 11:30 at the latest, we're in bed. We've had people to dinner. […]Usually on Sunday nights, following a tradition, John-John comes, a Brooklyn neighbor of Brett's whom Zach adores. In the next days, we'll see others. Tonight, we're going to a housewarming party and then to a series of readings by Southern writers, which is being held to raise funds for the opponent of Jesse Helms, the reactionary Carolina senator. […]So, as you can see, it's not as though we're the little reclusive couple. But we do also enjoy being alone together.

You ask me about Brett and his family. Unfortunately, a crisis is brewing with his parents that is about to explode, caused by a lot of resentment on Brett's part due to their behavior. He has good relationships with his sister Barbara who lives in Ohio and has a daughter a couple of years older than Stefano with whom we spent a delightful weekend, and his other sister Leslie who lives in Israel and also has a daughter. His parents live in Philadelphia, quite near, but they never come to visit, and he suffers from this. About Brett, I have so much to say, but right now I don't feel like going into it. Anyway, he is extremely sweet, but even he has his mood swings and his quirks like everyone else, and he is very family oriented. Soon, I'll send you a photo and a more detailed description of his character and his personal story.

[...]I had lunch with Sam yesterday. [...]He is ambivalent about my relationship with Brett. Anyway, he hasn't yet met him or Zach and I am sure that as soon as he does, he'll be won over. (Zach, as Manu told you, is a sweetheart.)

And you, strength and courage! It's up to you. But there are also so many people who wish you well and are rooting for you, the first in line being your Gio.

P.S. Have you seen Stefano? What impression do you have? Are you considering arranging a weekly visit with him?

When Giovanni gave me the news that his T-4 cell count had dropped to 128, my grieving process began. There is something cold about a number. Its abstractness and irrefutability, its intangible quality are its power and give it power to inspire panic. In typical fashion, Giovanni underplayed its value as he told me over dinner in a restaurant. He treated the words as if they were merely interfering with the taste of the prosciutto he was eating. However, they chilled me completely. They translated immediately into, "I am starting to die." Each subsequent change in his condition, however small, was a crisis because the implied pronouncement was always the same: "I am continuing to die." New reminders, each equally as traumatizing as its predecessor, compelling us to remanipulate and forge a new routine, create a new rhythm, to eke a sense of normalcy out of our diminishing resources.

In late September, Giovanni introduced the idea of adopting another child. "Each of us has had our own. Raising an infant together would be the ultimate bond between us," he explained to me. I believed him, but I also believe that while Giovanni was still arguably asymptomatic, the sporadic bouts of diarrhea, the waning but as yet manageable loss of energy, and the slight decline in his T-4 cell count were beginning to have the cumulative power to erode Giovanni's belief that he was going to be the first AIDS victim not to die of AIDS. His illness was no longer undercover. It was now causing us to make modifications, however slight or easily assimilated, to our days. There was a viable threat to his life, which gave him audacity. An infant, a bud of life, to subsume or cancel out the ember of death. Or at least to help him to continue to forget that he was dying. The child would be our bond, for a while our hope, and in the end our legacy. I agreed to think about it, and in spite of the fact that my mental gyrations produced nothing but anxiety(the most obvious concern being: How can I possibly take care of a three-year-old, an infant, and Giovanni? Another being that only a few weeks before, I had left my full-time job for a part-time job with the idea of using my two extra free days to begin teaching and freelance writing again), I agreed to proceed with the adoption. The hours of paperwork and phone calls began and served as a cushion between me and the question, "Why am I doing this?"

New York, Friday, October 5

Dearest Emanuela,

My second try. My first letter, written on the computer, was obliterated by Zach, who put crackers in the disk drive, thinking it was a toaster (Uh oh!) [...]Oh, I love you, dear sister. You and Flaminia are among the reasons that I feel homesick for Rome. And now, obviously, and in first place, Stefano.

[...]Brett and I went through a tempestuous period, discussing the possibility of adopting a second child (I would like a girl). He is very anxious that, given my health situation, I might be taking on too much. (It is true that I am ALWAYS tired and sleepy, but I believe it has more to do with the changes in my life than in the changes in my condition, even if it is true that my T4 cells dropped to 128, an all-time low.) Then his therapist said to him, "Don't think about whether Giovanni can or cannot handle another child, don't think about whether Zach would be jealous or happy to have a little brother, think only: I, Brett, do I want another child now?" And his reply was no. Anyway, he's already rethinking it. He is even more neurotic and uncertain than me! Yuk! Yuk!

A big hug, Gio.

6

New York, November 19, 1990

Dear Emanuela,

Just a few lines to thank you again for your hospitality before I leave again—tomorrow morning for San Francisco for Thanksgiving. I am a little terrified by the six-hour flight with Zach. He is not like Stefano (who always slept soundly from takeoff to touchdown). Speaking of Stefano, your tender loving care and Sara's presence made our stay in your apartment much more pleasant for him and comforting for me. Thank you, thank you, thank you.

As for the rest, I should be—I imagine—worried about the future with all the things that need to be done and the possibility of them getting stuck (will you be able to rent Mamma's Via Luciani apartment for 1991? The country house in Porvietoli for July and August? Where will Mamma be? Where will I, Brett, Stefano, Zach, and maybe the new baby be in the first months of 1992? (Auuuugh!) But in reality, I am not worried. Maybe I'm irresponsible or maybe I trust in destiny. As for the rest, with my health condition, one needs to be a bit fatalistic. To try to control the future is a delirious ambition for anyone but especially for me.

Brett was a little tense upon my return from Italy because I didn't give him enough attention and wanted to read the newspapers and the mail. But soon he got over it with a night of sparks and fireworks! Tomorrow we're going to the theatre to see *Six Degrees of Separation* (tickets were bought in July—this to show you how things work in Anglo-Saxon countries). Tomorrow morning, we leave, and it will be a wonderful vacation with Brett's two friends Ann and Nicky (we'll stay with them), my friend Giovanni Vitiello, and our cousins Livia and Daniel. Brett and I will be together all day without any of the usual chores or errands, and it will be great. Come to think of it, it's the first vacation that we are having together!

Zach didn't grow unaccustomed to me during my ten-day absence, and he is as affectionate and lively as always. The ties grow stronger every day. He is exhausting (last night at ten o'clock a friend called, and I was already sound asleep!), but so cheering. He helps me to feel Stefano's absence less.

[...]A kiss, Gio.

Throughout our vacation in San Francisco, Giovanni slept an inordinate amount. He would wake in the late morning, take a long nap in the afternoon, and fall asleep every evening by 9:30. He assured me that he was always hypersensitive to jet lag, and what with this double trip covering nine time zones, he was suffering the phenomenon at its extreme. I wanted to believe his diagnosis.

When we returned to New York, he never fully recovered. Naps became imperative, and evenings together grew shorter. When I emerged from Zach's room after having put him to bed, I'd usually find Giovanni on the sofa fast asleep. We decided that Giovanni would no longer wake up to an alarm clock but rather would wake up when his body told him to. The body clock always roused him after Zach's departure for school, and this special time for Giovanni and Zach came to an end. Giovanni also stopped waking up on Sundays with Zach as it seemed to slow him down for the rest of the day. Our weekend threesomes in the playground petered out as well. Zach and I would venture out while Giovanni stayed behind to take his nap. Sometimes he would join us later, sometimes not. I was finding myself increasingly having to take care of two people rather than one, both with entirely different needs and sleeping schedules. I was either alone with Zach or playing with Zach while Giovanni was in the background. On rare and lucky days, if Giovanni had a long and late nap, he would be able to stay up beyond Zach's bedtime and we'd have an hour or so alone together in the evening.

When Giovanni was asleep in the mornings or afternoons, I always felt obliged to take Zach out of the apartment. On weekends Zach and I would be outdoors by 7:30 in the morning, Zach riding around the neighborhood on his tricycle, making pit stops to collect stones, jump off apartment stoops, or visit the local gas station where there was a jelly bean machine and a Pakistani attendant who let Zach help him put the hose in the gas tanks of the cars. We'd return home at 10:30, at which time I'd make breakfast. I was already beginning to ebb and I knew that I had only a few precious hours of Giovanni's company before I'd be on my own again, exiled from the house with Zach.

I hated the weekends. They were solitary, tedious, unfair. Even when I joined forces with other parents, I couldn't help but think about what was unable to exist in my relationship with Giovanni. On those occasions when I was in the world of healthy, energetic couples, such as at parties or at the playground, I was overpowered by the contrast. I was envious of each and every one of them; even if there wasn't an equal distribution of responsibilities, there was, in some measure, a sharing of responsibilities. No, I was not envious of them, I was envious of their potential as couples. I imagined one playing with the baby while the other prepared dinner or one going to the grocery store while the other put weather-stripping around the windows; I imagined the end of their day, the child asleep and they alone together, finally, frazzled, looking at each other and recognizing the communal exhaustion of mutual effort, and the droplet of bond-glue that would ensue. I felt cheated and bereft. Still, at this point, the presence of the illness was only evidenced by a lack of energy or, rather, a need to sleep. And I was sufficiently uninformed about AIDS to think that this lethargy could be temporary or was at least treatable with proper nutrition and lots of rest.

When Giovanni was awake, he was always physically and mentally engaged. He was one of life's great enthusiasts and denied his illness to the fullest extent possible. He didn't hesitate to invite people to the house at a time when he knew his body would be aching for a nap; neither did he take inventory of his medications to assure that he had enough for the weekend, nor ask his doctor questions during his regular six-week checkup. He wanted to have nothing to do with his illness and he believed that he could starve it out of his body through a combination of neglect, defiance, and optimism. I, on the other hand, felt most comfortable when I believed that I had some measure of control over it, and my sense of control was accrued through diligent oversight of Giovanni's sleep, weight, diet, medications, and any and all information I could get my hands on pertaining to experimental studies underway. It was only a matter of time before I was preparing meticulously balanced meals three times a day and pureed high-calorie protein concoctions in the evening, meting out his pills, sending him off to bed at the least suggestion of a yawn, and having private consultations with his doctor in order to understand and anticipate all that Giovanni had no interest in understanding or anticipating. There were frequent arguments about our polar approaches to his illness, but I believe that secretly each of us was grateful to the other for providing a kind of equilibrium to a situation that could have cinched us in a mental vise long before its physical components closed in. Our motives were identical: to somehow make the menace go away.

In November, I had one of my last "bachelor" evenings out. My best friend, who was also HIV positive, and I had dinner in a restaurant in the Village. He had brought with him a folder of information describing an experimental treatment that was being conducted in a private clinic in Switzerland for people with HIV or AIDS. The treatment itself was quite simple, nontoxic, and expensive. One pint of the patient's blood is removed, mixed with carceranum, treated with ozone, and injected back into the bloodstream. This treatment is administered on three successive days and requires half-hour visits to the clinic. Additionally, the patient takes Rovital-V drops and gel and intramuscular injections of Carciviren at home over a period of six months.

The results to date had been very promising, the patients gradually reverting back to an asymptomatic state as their T-4 cell counts increased. I brought the information home with me and let it sit for a while in a box that I'd started for such treatments. Within a month, three other people had mentioned the treatment to me, and so I began to investigate it more thoroughly, first, by calling many of the patients who had undergone the treatment. The more inquiries I made, the more hopeful I became. I spoke to Giovanni about it, and we decided that we would submit an application and try to get an appointment for the week after we arrived in Rome. Our only fear was that for one week prior to the treatment and for the duration of the treatment, all other medications had to be suspended since they were incompatible with the medications comprising the Swiss cure. Although Beedie was a chafing reminder of the virus, it also housed what was purported to be the chemical hocus-pocus that slowed it down. The prospect of retiring the magic coffer was frightening, indeed. After all, nothing was definitive, everything brushed up against controversy if one did enough research, as one doctor's opinion canceled out another's; in the end, decisions had to be more or less a gamble based on such unscientific factors as instinct, degree of comfort, willingness to take risks. When I was completing the application the following October to be faxed to Switzerland, I recall having had a vivid but fleeting image of Groucho Marx. I couldn't make any connection to this image until, several days later, when discussing it in therapy, I remembered that he hosted a television show called, *You Bet Your Life*.

New York, Friday, November 30, 1990

Dear Donatella [Giovanni's stepmother],

I found this letter, which I never sent, [...]in my briefcase. We went to San Francisco for a wonderful Thanksgiving vacation. The weather was perfect. We had Thanksgiving dinner in a beautiful house in the Oakland hills with a view of the bay, a breathtaking flaming sunset, the Golden Gate Bridge and the silhouette of the city.

[...]These days I am often tired for no particular reason and at night I sleep nine, ten, even eleven hours (two times I slept for thirteen). Back pains and some stomach problems contribute to my not feeling in great shape, hardly being creative, and even less disciplined. The simultaneous publication of two books written by my friends has not helped this sense of lacking a purpose, of wasting my talents in a magazine that NO

ONE I know reads (except faithful Nonna Maria who continues to buy it every week). But the subjects that I could write about overwhelm me, and the amount of work that would be necessary to produce a book that isn't shoddy, banal, casual, or contrived frightens me even more. I don't know if I am capable of doing it. I feel lacking in energy, and I contribute far less than 50 percent toward the necessary domestic work; fortunately, Brett is very active and caring and he can do the shopping, cooking, dishwashing, and tend to Zach all in ten minutes while I lie back on the sofa to read the newspaper or watch the news on TV. What's more, since he shifted to part-time work he has begun to write, and now he is moving like a train. (And I am a little envious.) Bah, I shouldn't allow myself these blues. In part, I am saddened by Mamma's situation, and Stefano's distance weighs heavily. The day after tomorrow is his birthday, the first in which I will not be participating.

[...]Enough with my complaints, which are really unjustifiable. Write soon. A big hug, Gio.

New York, Saturday, January 5, 1991

Dear Mamma and Emanuela,

Stefano left today. His much longed for visit passed in a flash. I am a bit sad, but I am also content because the visit went really well. I was afraid that he would be jealous of Zach or of having to share his room or that he wouldn't get along well with Brett or that the distance would have changed something in our relationship. Instead, everything was better. Stefano is truly golden, loving, accommodating, and basically obedient. His defects (he doesn't want to work, eats like a pig, is lazy) are easily corrected and, anyway, wouldn't alter his personality. He was playful with Zach, and his relationship with Brett deepened. A lot of this is to Brett's credit. He gave Stefano a lot of attention and care, at the same time telling him clearly and without hesitation what he thought of some of his attitudes and asking him to do things (hang up his jacket, clear the table, etc.). With only a little arguing and some negotiating, we got him to do his homework almost every day and to take a shower every other day. His obsession with video games and television was under control, even if it was kind of pointless to do so for ten days in New York when there is no limit when he's in Rome. Brett was horrified when Stefano told him that Giovanna spends even more time in front of the Nintendo than him! [...]One thing is certain: he felt loved. When he arrived, there were lots of colored balloons on the walls and a streamer hanging from the ceiling that said, "Welcome back." And last night we had our farewell dinner in a restaurant. When dessert came, the waiter brought a cake with a candle and the inscription, "Buon viaggio. We'll miss you." I think that on the whole he found the house more inviting than when he was alone with me because it was more lively and because Brett was so caring, cooking a wonderful dinner every night instead of the crap that I used to do (like order a pizza and eat it in front of the TV). It's not that he was monopolized by us either. He saw his friend Paul once (snowball fight and a movie), and several times he went to Matthew's house (generally to play video games to death). Both of them came to the house too. I was afraid that he would be embarrassed by the new situation, but he seemed unfazed by it. Both Sam and Stefano's ex-violin teacher showed their affection: Sam driving for two hours (he now lives in the country) to come to the city to spend an entire day with him, and John, who works in a bank, taking the subway to come downtown during his lunch break to eat with all of us in a restaurant in Tribeca.

[...]Dear Mamma, both Brett and I are thrilled about your arrival. Our life is a little lackluster and domestic, perhaps, but I don't think that you're expecting or even wanting fireworks. It's been so long since we've seen each other, and we'll have time to talk and to catch up. And if I can be helpful for your "internal" work to confront your problems from the bottom, so much the better; and vice versa, maybe, I'll confront my Oedipus!

Did Flami get my little birthday present through Stefano? Give her a big hug from me and Sara and Andrea, and a big kiss for you from Gio.

With the adoption process initiated and moving forward on its own momentum, Giovanni and I discussed the possibility of getting married. We thought to have a traditional (as much as tradition would permit) Jewish wedding in a synagogue, followed by a small reception in our apartment. Despite our mutual desire to keep it inexpensive and modest, the preparations nevertheless required the same hours and amount of detail work as a more elaborate wedding. My recently acquired "days off" consisted of dashing all over the city talking to rabbis, studying traditional Jewish wedding contracts and ceremonies in the library; shopping for rings, yarmulkes, tallith; meeting with caterers, printers, photographers, and, whenever I happened to pass an untried pharmacy or apothecary along the way, stopping in to stock up on the various protein liquids and homeopathic medicines with which we were supplementing Giovanni's professionally prescribed treatment. Resentment was beginning to fester. There was a gross imbalance in the division of labor and sharing of responsibility. I was becoming harried by my own efficiency. I tried to attribute the imbalance to Giovanni's illness, but I knew that my own tendency to take charge played a significant part, as well as Giovanni's general aversion to responsibility. It was futile to try and distinguish between those activities in which Giovanni did not participate because of his illness and those activities in which he didn't participate out of laziness. Giovanni barely acknowledged the existence of his illness, so it was impossible for him to speak of its day-to-day consequences. This was the source of our greatest conflict, and until he was bedridden and the distinction became crystal clear, we were never able to resolve it.

 A wedding, a newborn, these strivings to coax the best and the strongest from tradition into an unorthodox setting were a dare to the world and a dare to death. The unspoken sentiment and conviction—and desperate hope—was that AIDS, which usually made its incursions into the more marginal segments of society, would find itself bored or out of its element or suddenly sympathetic, and would just leave, as if it were a murderer whose wisp of a soul could be appealed to. Part of Giovanni couldn't help but be drawn into the belief that AIDS was his punishment for promiscuity, and if only he could redeem himself, the punishment would be lifted. I have no doubt that had Giovanni not been sick we would have been married and had more children, but the decisions would certainly have been slower in the making and the reasons would not have had as their mooring the idea of exorcising a malevolence. For, at bottom, these two projects were just that: moorings to which we devoted ourselves in order to verify an idea that we wanted to keep alive, namely that Giovanni's virus was not going to swell into AIDS, that Giovanni was not going to die.

Giovanni's mother, Silvia, arrived in the middle of January, soon after Stefano left, and spent six weeks with us. An extremely intelligent, perceptive, and emotionally fragile woman, she had recently gone through her own personal crises and arrived in New York with the expectation of being restored by our care to reasonable health, or at least being taken care of while she regained her strength. We gave her our bedroom and bathroom and slept on a miniature sofa bed in the living room and used the common bathroom in the hall. Giovanni continued to use our bedroom for his naps, and in the morning when Zach woke up, Giovanni would slip into Zach's room and finish his sleep.

Silvia was most anxious when her time was unstructured. If she woke up in the morning with nothing planned for the day, she went into a stultifying panic. Giovanni and I mapped out her days for her when we had to work; occasionally he would take a day off from work and spend it with her, and my two free days were always spent in her company, which was delightful. I was very happy to be getting to know what would soon be my family, and the closeness that Silvia and I established was immediate and free of the need for delicacy. On the other hand, I, as is my custom, took it upon myself to be responsible for her recuperation, and the pressure and resentment had even more fuel.

February 9, 1991

Dear Flaminia,

I am on the train from Port Jefferson to New York. I went there this morning with Mamma. I left her there with Angelica and she'll come back tomorrow afternoon. How is she? She has many ups and downs. It's been such a long time since she has been on my territory, and this is rather difficult for me. Brett is an angel and helps me out a great deal. He gives her lots of attention and isn't bothered by the fact that she is always present in what would otherwise be our moments alone. For example, on the night of my birthday, we all went out to dinner to a Tuscan restaurant. [...]And again on Valentine's Day the three of us are going to see *The Magic Flute*, with sets by David Hockney. Brett has extreme difficulties with his mother (in this period they are not speaking to each other), but with our mother he is so affectionate. Instead, he is upset with me, and, unfortunately, his complaints are ones that I have already heard from others in the past (and that therefore must surely contain elements of truth): that I am too focused on myself, that I don't pay attention to him, that I read the newspapers and then still have to watch the news while he is cooking and at the same time tending to Zach, that I let myself be served hand and foot, that sometimes he feels invisible . . . I am making a great effort to change my behavior, but it never seems to be enough. I love him so much, and I could even force myself not to turn on the TV, but the truth is that I would prefer to watch the news. Especially now. I realize that I have written a letter that is entirely personal, without any mention of the war or of my problems with *L'Espresso*, but maybe it is better this way. A big hug. Gio.

Saturday, March 2

Dear Emanuela,
    Happy belated birthday! I hope you liked my little

gift. I love the sweater that you and Flami got me for my birthday and I wear it often. It's a warm and gray afternoon. Mother is sleeping here in the living room, Zach in his bed, and Brett in our room where he put everything back in order with lightning speed as soon as Mother had packed. Everyone is sleeping, worn out by the explosive tensions of the last hours, due to an accumulation of factors: in part, the extension of mother's visit; in part, the personality and character differences and expectations between Brett and me: he a Cancer, clingy, dependent, domestic, crafty, organized, needing attention; I an Aquarius, vague, egocentric, disorganized, needing room to breathe. Last night we hardly slept. We argued until 2, then at 4 I woke up and we started up again, at 5:30 we tried to go back to sleep but: first, the cat made a shit in the litter box, scratching the sand incessantly; then the coffee in the automatic coffee machine in the kitchen started to brew (we were sleeping in the living room, where there is no door). Finally, a little after 6, Zach woke up and, at that point, I went in his room and slept until 10:30. Mamma was very upset by our fight, always blaming herself, of course, and saying, "On my very last day here," we mustn't do this.

[...]She is in strong competition with Zach for my attention and she says that I spoil him, but she also has had her tender moments with him.

All in all, I would say that she is better than when she arrived. The crises and anxiety attacks continue but she controls them better and she seems to understand that they will pass. What worries me is the deadly sadness that takes hold of her as soon as she has to spend a day alone. It's as if she doesn't have her own fuel and always needs to refuel herself from others.

The war is over, and no sense of comfort can be gotten from it. It was a tragedy, tens of thousands of poor Iraqis and Kuwaitis are dead, the oil wells will continue to burn for months with dire ecological consequences; the Gulf is contaminated. Still, it could have been a tragedy of incomparably greater proportions, hence, the relief. At the same time, it can't be said that roots of the violence have been removed: avarice, tyranny, exploitation, imperialism, inequality, demagoguery, fundamentalism, and nationalism. How much time before another Saddam Hussein springs forth? You know how much I was in favor of the UN and the idea of a world government. But I'm not so thrilled about the way it has kicked off. On the other hand, the aggression in Kuwait cannot go unpunished. As you see, I have contradictory thoughts and feelings, but it's been like this for me since the beginning of this war.

Monday, we'll have news from the adoption agency in Texas. If the biological father agrees to relinquish his rights, we'll have a baby in little over a month. Half-German, half-Black! I'm full of expectations even if Brett wisely exhorts me to not let go of the reins until we are sure. When we know the date, and now that the war is over, I'd like to come for a week to see Stefano. Stefano is coming to NY for a week for the wedding (tentative date June 23), and we'd be thrilled if you could come too. Then, in July, he is going to Africa with Giovanna and in August will return here where we'll rent a house on Fire Island where I'll stay with the children and Brett will go back and forth to New York to work.

A big hug, Gio.

Aside from the enjoyable adult company, Silvia's visit gave me a strong sense of what life would be like with a third person in the household whom I'd primarily be doing things "for" rather than "with." Silvia had become one more field of need, and I saw, and felt, the results of her visit on my nervous system as well as on my relationship with Giovanni. I was stretched (at least I thought so at the time), and this effort to provide care in superhuman bounty set off a series of explosions and internal conflicts that led me to a support group and, ultimately, to a decision to put off the adoption. The latter decision, however, was not made before Silvia had accompanied me to Long Island where a social worker was conducting the adoption home study. By including Silvia in the process, I was hoping to make her more amenable to the idea and in so doing to give the desire to adopt at least a modicum of credibility outside of the world of Giovanni and me. While Silvia did seem to grow more enthusiastic about the adoption by the end of the home study, she also chose this occasion, as we were walking back to the train station, to talk to me at great length about when she discovered that Giovanni was HIV positive and how she has since lived with this knowledge. I think it was her way of saying to me, "Think carefully about this undertaking. Remember the context in which you are carrying it out."

The former resolve—to join a support group—was welcomed by Giovanni. The latter—to put a halt to the adoption—was a bludgeon to his soul. It took me some time to prepare myself to tell Giovanni that I thought it best to suspend the adoption. I knew that he would take it hard, primarily because of its metaphorical import. With the exception of eating sushi and shellfish, there was nothing in Giovanni's life that had had to be eliminated altogether. Activities narrowed incrementally, were modified, took longer, but never ceased to exist. The infant, however, had to cease to exist. It couldn't be in our life part-time, when Giovanni was feeling up to it, and I didn't have it in me to take it on single-handedly while Giovanni provided a background glow. The infant no longer had the power to push AIDS out of our household. I had to sink it or be sunk, knowing that for Giovanni it would represent the first unequivocal surrender. When the moment was ripe, Giovanni and I were sitting on the sofa. I took his hands. Two hours later, the infant was dead, taking with it a part of Giovanni as vital to him as any anatomical target AIDS would zoom in on and destroy.

7

New York, April 1, 1991

Dear Emanuela,

Days of emotional ups and downs reflected in the extremely variable weather. One day it is 77 degrees, hot, windows open, people in T-shirts. The next day the temperature drops suddenly, and by dawn of the next day, it is snowing! We've had two extremely cold and rainy days, and every so often, huge winds sweep away the clouds and one can see the sun.

My physical and emotional state is not good. I am always tired and inefficient. The limit was reached between Friday and Saturday. Friday night I had a fever of 101 (I know this number means nothing to you). I went to bed early and slept twelve hours. The next day at noon there was a weekly yoga lesson for people with HIV, not far from the house where I've already gone twice with beneficial results. I was getting ready to go, around 11:30 when I realized that I just couldn't. I was exhausted and wouldn't have been able to do a thing. Brett encouraged me to go back to sleep (he told me afterward that my face was so drawn that it was frightening), and so I did. I get tired walking and even more so going up stairs. I take a nap whenever I have a chance, regardless of whether the previous night I slept ten hours (which is now the norm for me). I almost always take a taxi to work, giving in to the fatigue and to the lure of being able to put it on *L'Espresso*'s account. In short, I am turning into James Revson and in precisely those behaviors for which I criticized him most.

The mention of James Revson is not casual. I had news about him from Sam. It's not good. He is in the hospital with PCP. He absolutely does not want me to see him and is very bitter about me. My reaction on learning this news was panic, not for noble reasons, I fear, but all selfish. For whom does the bell toll? I am next. I am being treated by the same doctor as James is, I take the same medications, among which Bactrim is supposed to prevent PCP. I can't even go to see him and I feel completely powerless. This is the beginning of the end, and I wouldn't want him to depart before being able to tell him how sorry I am for the bad that I unwillingly caused. But if this is the beginning of the end for him, why not for me? Only because I am several steps behind. I am like he was one year ago (with the exception of KS, which is certainly a big difference). Philosophically, we are all heading in the same direction, but the speed is not the same. Maybe I should have resigned myself when I was diagnosed HIV positive, but, apparently, I kept a magic hope (expectation) that the medications would save me. Now this certainty is shaken, and for the first time, I am clearly not in control of my body. All this does nothing to help my rather depressed mood. Everything seems flat, predictable, disconnected.

Mamma's decision to not proceed with our plan to buy two apartments [from the sale of her apartment] was a horrible shock for me, as much for practical reasons as for emotional ones. From the practical point of view, I am worried that I will have to make do with a drastic reduction in my salary and, furthermore, will find myself in a small, cramped apartment in the periphery that is still extremely expensive. I feel tremendously guilty with respect to Brett, that I am dragging him into this adventure of our move to Rome since the results could be very different than what I was expecting. [...]I have to base myself substantially on my resources and I feel that these are dwindling. I am grateful for your idea [of us moving in with you] and hope very much that it can be done, but I have to be careful not to invest you with images of a surrogate mother because that is precisely what you're trying to get away from with all of your energy and I don't want to be the one, of course, to nail you down. You can show this letter to Flami if you think it's appropriate.

A big, big hug, Gio.

Tuesday, April 9

Dear Brett:

I'm finally writing you the letter that I promised a long time ago. I know you're unsatisfied with our level of communication, but it's too upsetting for me to talk about certain things in person, so maybe writing is a better idea. This morning Emanuela called, she wanted to know how I am doing, and as soon as I started telling her, I choked up and I had to fight back tears. I can't afford this to happen with you. She was very stern, said I should ban negative thoughts completely, and I should thank God for all the good things

He sent me: you in the first place. And also, she said, you need to take naps? Be grateful that you CAN and leave it at that. She sounded relieved (from the burden of our mother) and energetic, she's seriously studying Reiki (I don't know if this is the right spelling), and the next step will be "mental" and she wants to treat me from afar; she'll tell me the time and I'll have to lie down on the sofa and be relaxed. I don't believe in this crap in the least, but if it makes her happy, I'll do it. Good news also about Flaminia: she has been awarded a free trip to Vienna and Budapest because she's such a good worker.

I'm sitting in the area outside the Bleecker Street Playground. The company is not exactly uplifting. Some black men are sleeping. Some older white guys are reading. Some emaciated white guys are sitting, staring into space. A guy with very long hair, who arrived seeming reasonably masculine, is now putting makeup on his face, looking at himself in a special magnifying mirror in a frenzy of gestures (wait, he just got up and left). It's not as pleasant as it was the last few days. It's muggy and cloudy and somehow the warmth feels less healthy.

An old queen with dyed red hair just sat next to me, and I would like to go away but I also want to write to you. Unfortunately, I don't seem to be able to elevate myself beyond the immediate and the anecdotal, which is not what I had in mind.

I guess the words I have to tell you are very hard to utter, even in writing. First of all, I want to tell you how much I love you, what a big difference you have made in my life, and how I hate the idea of leaving you. But we have to be grown-ups and face every possibility, especially because we have responsibilities toward other people (in your case, Zach). I can't take my mind off the vision of you stranded in Italy alone with one or two children (one of the black homeless men just woke up). What could you do? I doubt that my family and friends could give you more than token help. Adding to this the grief and the sorrow, it could be devastating. I think that before the actual move, we have to give a hard look at my health situation and decide. I can't bear the idea of facing anything without you at my side, so maybe I should stay. I mean: the goal of our move is to be with Stefano but what if I won't have the energy? More: should I expose him to actually witness while his Dad goes? Maybe that's not fair and it would run counter to what we think he needs. Emanuela would probably say that those are negative thoughts, but I think they are just realistic. He'd be heartbroken if I didn't go, but we know that he'd be even more heartbroken in the future. It's a no-win situation. I'm not saying we should decide anything now but in December we should be open to any option. The only option I can't consider is to separate from you. I know it's selfish.

I know that you are being sexually deprived and I think we should change certain things in the organization of our days (especially the days when you don't work) to allow us to spend some precious time together. Maybe we'll have to lower our expectations as to the degree of passion involved, but what really matters is the affection we share. The other night, even if I didn't participate and had my eyes closed and on the outside I was totally passive, I knew you could feel my love flowing toward you and that's why it was satisfactory for you. But I know that you'll need more and I suggest that we try and spend time together some afternoon.

Right now, our home is not very inviting, what with the workers tearing down walls to replace pipes. "Big men" as Zach would say. They're totally dismantling it, and I feel violated. I'm realizing once more that in this letter I'm not expressing my feelings toward you, which was its purpose. Maybe I've some kind of block. Can you read between the lines? Can you guess the intensity of my love even if I don't spell it out? I hope so. See, after all, I'm more similar to my father than I thought. I'm also probably afraid to break down even by myself in this park if I just write certain words and concepts so I avoid them and, once more, I let you do all the work of interpretation.

Maybe instead of you going to a support group alone, we should go together to a group where I would be encouraged to express my feelings. (A long line of handicapped people proceeds on the sidewalk, one of them screams like a bird at regular intervals. My Beedie goes off and I take my four blue pills without any water.) Emanuela says it's going to be very difficult for her to rent in the country. Buying would be much easier, but for that she'd have to sell her apartment, so forget that solution too. Rome appears increasingly unwelcoming for us.

My dearest Brett, I don't think it's fair to ask you to give more than you can, to stretch your strength to its extreme limits. I think you need to take some distance from me. I don't know how. Most of all, I mean emotional distance. Kind of starting to let go. I know it's hard, it's even harder for me. (Four construction workers arrived and are having their lunch on a bench nearby, one of them has a T-shirt that says "Masonry

Pro" on one side and "Buscarello" on the other. They all wear caps; no one has a hairband.) The world seems predictable today but in a warm, comforting way. I like the fact that construction workers look like construction workers. In a way, it frees you up. I wonder what other people see when they look at me. You think one of those emaciated guys? I hope not. Those appeared to have lost much more weight than me. By the way, Philip was in great shape last night. I see I'm rambling again, so I better stop here and go have some lunch, maybe at the Penguin Cafe.

I love you very much, G.

I tried to
"think
kink"
Bretty,
but I could
"think
pink"
only!
What can I do if a lovely
perverse thought doesn't enter my mind?
Would you be satisfied only
if I tied you up and things of the kind?
A quiet, warm conjugal embrace
(without even wearing panties of lace)
is what I actually crave for.
I guess I'm a romantic and a bore.

New York, Thursday, April 25

Dear Emanuela,
It's a beautiful sunny morning with a fresh breeze

every once in a while. I am sitting on a bench in Father Demo Square at the intersection of Bleecker, Carmine, and Sixth Avenue. Later, probably after lunch, I will rent a car, and when Brett returns from work, we will leave for Philadelphia. We'll spend the night at his parents' house, so I'll see where he grew up, and the following morning we will head out for our little weekend in the country (we've already made a reservation in New Hope for Friday night but not for Saturday).

Yesterday at 2:00 we went to see *Mery per Sempre*, and the boys from Palermo reminded me so much of the blacks in the urban ghettos here. One difference: for each time that they say "cock" the ones here say "shit." What will there be, anthropologically speaking, behind this different emphasis on genital and excretory functions? In any case, they are boys without hope, their destiny is sealed, and they themselves don't seem in any way able to conceive of a way out. This tragic resemblance makes one understand that the main problem is not skin color, as here it is always made out to be, but the socio-economic conditions and the culture of violence, of abuse, and of desperation. Having said these words, the only serious and logical thing to do would be to do volunteer work in these ghettos, more so someone like me who has the guarantee of a salary without work. Instead, I do nothing.

I am a little uncomfortable because yesterday I sent Mamma a letter that was perhaps too harsh. Nothing that you and I haven't said dozens of times, but irrevocably written and sent to her, these words seem almost merciless, and I wonder if I haven't done harm by writing on the impulse of the moment. On the telephone with her and with you, I was instead able to be balanced (apart from that nasty phrase, "I'll come to visit you from Magliana"). It's stupid to hurt her when by this time I know that it doesn't push her to change. In addition, it is even a little suspect, this sudden inflexibility of mine, right when her decisions strike at my interests. It's not that she could be otherwise. It is just that I wasn't comfortable telling her those things. But a grudge is always a bad counselor, besides being poison for the soul.

Here in the square, there are a lot of nice elderly men who are chatting (I imagine that the elderly women are at home cooking) and a couple of babies in strollers. From this observation point, New York certainly doesn't make one think of the swarmy ant hill that many compare it to. Even the traffic isn't terrible. And the quality of the air is better than in Rome (which doesn't say much).

[...]Brett is very optimistic and flexible about our move to Rome. He says that everything will work out fine, whether it be in the country or whatever neighborhood in the city (but he is used to public transportation that works). He even decided to look for work from here and, if he succeeds, to start immediately upon our arrival. This displeases me a little because I know that he would prefer to have time to "absorb" the city, but maybe it is necessary. Anyway, if the dollar continues to rise, his monthly profit from his house (after deducting the mortgage, maintenance, and a fund for repairs) will be worth more and more in lire.

Now I have a hunch that very, very slowly, like a little old man, I will make my way to the house, stopping at the Italian bakery for a cannolo. I'll take a nap soon so that I'll have time to go and rent the car.

I miss Stefano so much and am always anxious to hear his news.[...]

A big affectionate hug, Gio.

The trip to New Hope was a confluence of flashpoints. We planned to drive to my parents' house, one hour from New Hope, and spend the night with them: Giovanni was going to make his debut in the suburban setting of the first sixteen years of my life. In addition, we were leaving Zach with my parents for the weekend: Giovanni and I were going to have two child-free days for the first time since we had met. Perhaps most important, at least for me, was the fact that this prolonged visit with my parents required that I broach the subject of Giovanni's condition, which had reached a point where it—or at least a suspicion of something in the vicinity of it—was visible to anyone who spent more than a few hours with him. I was chilled at the prospect of telling my parents, far more so than the friends whom I had already told; unlike my friends, whose sympathy and concern instantaneously embraced both Giovanni and me, my parents' predatory instinct would assure that the filaments of their emotional authority repelled Giovanni while cleaving to their son with the discomfort and weight of damp clothes. "Why didn't you run in the other direction when you found out?" It was a question that would begin to rise inside me whenever fear, despair, and physical exhaustion combined to topple me, but as long as the words didn't have a resounding echo from without, they were easily subdued in the larger pool of thought. I told my parents about a week before we were to arrive. They did ask the question and, moreover, the tone of their voices revealed consternation more than care. The subtext was, "Oy, how could you be so stupid?" when what I needed from them, and knew I couldn't possibly get, was more along the lines of,

"Oh, honey, what can we do to help?" Fortunately, the weeklong grace period was sufficient for their reaction and my reaction to their reaction, to soften. They were, and continued to be, verbally solicitous if in absentia.

New Hope is a rural community situated on the Delaware River, midway between New York and Philadelphia. A haven to once-urban artists, it is culturally vibrant and visually rustic, though its theme of quaintness is somewhat overbaked. Giovanni and I stayed outside of the village proper in a large guesthouse that was formerly the Oscar Hammerstein estate festooned with Hammerstein memorabilia and surrounded by farmland and forests. My expectations were as high as they were spurious: stripped of all responsibilities, schedules, and psychological wear-and-tear, Giovanni's energy level and sexual fervor would make a diffident comeback. We took short walks in the woods, along the canals, and in the center of the village; long drives along the Delaware River; and found simple restaurants for all our meals. Each outing, regardless of how unstrenuous, had to be couched within a one- or two-hour nap, during which time I would sit outside and read or take my own solitary walks. Moreover, in the evenings, Giovanni's impotence proved to be incontrovertible. It could no longer be construed as the combination of the illness plus a rough day at the office, or the illness plus the general weariness after a few hours with Zach. It was clear that the illness alone was sufficient to exhaust Giovanni after one or two hours of being awake, was sufficient alone to prevent him from being able to make love. The weekend retreat was my anti-utopian harbinger. I knew that Giovanni was never going to get better and that, for the duration of our relationship, it was never going to be better than this attenuated weekend, that, in fact, it was only going to grow worse.

And again, as always, a glimmer of hope. Upon our return

from New Hope, we went to Giovanni's doctor, who felt certain that the ambiguous efficacy of AZT had run its course and suggested that Giovanni suspend its use and replace it with an experimental drug called DDI. When I asked why he wasn't recommending DDC, another experimental drug with a longer history of ambiguous efficacy, the doctor told me that DDC could be given only to people who had AIDS, and Giovanni did not figure among them. This semantic nuance was a salve. In addition, while waiting for the doctor in the lounge, we had run into an acquaintance of Giovanni's who had begun the same treatment under the same physical conditions about two months before. He had more than gained back the weight he'd lost, was, in fact, plump, and his energy level had been restored, with the exception of an occasional afternoon nap, and who couldn't use one of those from time to time? We left the doctor's office cautiously elated. As so often happened when a facet of the condition had been diagnosed and a symptom-specific treatment recommended, we were able to forget, as in a kind of aphasia, that the symptom was merely one in a variable but ever-darkening spectrum of symptoms that made up the syndrome itself; instead, we could briefly disconnect the symptom from its temporal chain and think of it as an end in itself, as a discrete illness which was being treated and could possibly be cured.

Within two months, this confusion was set aright. Giovanni's condition continued to deteriorate at the same pace. A few harsh and ugly terms entered my personal AIDS lexicon, ones that I never dared let Giovanni hear. On a solo visit to Giovanni's doctor two months after he'd begun DDI, I was told that Giovanni was suffering from "wasting syndrome," a hideously accurate clinical appellative. The other terms required no doctor's consultation. Giovanni had been reduced to an invalid; I had been transformed into a housewife. Their resonance lay not in the future where there was already a surfeit of anxiety-producing statistics and probabilities waiting to pounce but in the present where they washed over Giovanni like an ebbless tide, an overall condition without components to be treated in isolation. Moreover, Giovanni's acquaintance, in the throes of his DDI comeback, had died of a brain fungus. Perhaps wrongly, I never told Giovanni.

8

New York, May 12 (Mother's Day)

Dear Emanuela,

It's a warm Sunday in May. Brett and Zach went to New Jersey to a baby-naming for the daughter of Brett's best friend—not really a baptism, given that they are Jewish. I wanted to go too, but yesterday I was out all day and was exhausted. My left leg hurts too much when I walk, and my lower back hurts anyway, even when I am lying down. Sometimes I think that Nature knows what she is doing. If I am not able to reach old age, she is letting me experience some of its conditions. Maybe it is necessary that one's participation in the external world narrows so you can focus spiritually and be ready for the great adventure. The problem, however, is that, contrary to what those who are truly old think (or what we imagine the truly old think), I don't really feel ready at all. Mainly, as you can imagine, because of Stefano and Zach, but above all—this may surprise you—because of Brett. In fact, I think that in these years Stefano has internalized a strong paternal image, and Zach has developed an affectionate relationship with me, but not one that is central (he is completely fixed on Brett). With Brett, on the other hand, despite his being an adult, it seems that he'd take this loss much worse. For example, my impotence. It is something that happened in the last weeks or months. It started with my not being able to have an orgasm (already at that point he was so upset that a few times I thought about faking it to please him), but soon it became a complete inability to have an erection. When I say complete, I mean not even in the morning when I wake up or under a hot shower or when I see a cute boy. I tried to masturbate: nothing. Not a quiver, a shake, a slight swelling. Now, what I must confess is that I don't care. In fact, I feel almost relieved. Even here, Nature—or the unconscious, if you prefer—played its little trick, removing on its own that which is the cause of my present condition. Indeed, but in reality, it isn't so simple. It could only be if I were single, something that I certainly don't want, and I could close the book on sex without regret. But there is Brett, who gives me everything and to whom I give so little in return. It would be truly cruel to deprive him of sex only because I am not interested, not so much for the thing in itself as much as because for him—and even for me—it is an important emotional connection. So, we do other things, and you might think that these alternatives would be more satisfying to him if he were a more traditional male since now it is obviously his member that is at the center of attention. But it isn't the case, and he misses our former practices so much. I even vaguely and confusedly thought to go to a sexual therapist, but we aren't really convinced. We don't want to undertake too many things at the same time because soon I will begin to participate in a support group.

    Another bit of good news is that I started to read

again. I just finished *The Mill on the Floss* by George Eliot (good but not comparable to her masterpiece *Middlemarch*) and I started Jude the Obscure by Thomas Hardy. I alternated them with essays by Cynthia Ozick and *The Soccer War* by a Polish journalist who was a correspondent abroad for many years. [...]I continue to go to yoga faithfully every Saturday, and yesterday there was someone there who was so distressingly thin that it broke my heart. Speaking of which, other good news: it seems that my weight loss has stopped (let's keep our fingers crossed). I look all right, but Brett says that it shows, especially when I am tired. In effect, now that we are approaching the fateful day, I might choose not to have the wedding. Not for the union with Brett, with whom I am more connected than ever, but for the stress and the expense and the obligation to appear in shape. (I don't want people to gossip behind my back.) It's already certain to me that when we move to Italy, we will not have the party that we had planned. It all has to do with the narrowing of horizons, which is not necessarily a bad thing. Maybe it helps one to see the beauty in a flower without the need of the forest. Speaking of forests, Brett thinks that in Rome we should live in the country, possibly with you, but I am hesitant. In particular, for Stefano, since I want him to have easy access to school from my house. I admit something a little shameful: I feel that I have more say about this subject because the money comes primarily from me. It's mean, I know, but think: Brett does absolutely everything, to the extent that even when I do something simple, like wash Zach's face and hands, he finds something wrong and redoes it. All the signs indicate that my dependence on him, even physical, will be increasing progressively. The only area in which I have autonomy is my income, and I am not afraid because in Italy it takes a lifetime before you can lose a job for health reasons. It's one of the good things about the Italian system that we should remember. But I don't know legally how I could transfer the liquidation to B. Enough, it's too premature to talk about this and a little morbid as well. I wish to reach a state of serenity and acceptance, but for now, I am quite far away from that. I fear that I am paying for the years squandered in worldly interests [...]rather than concentrating on my spiritual growth. Now I have to do a crash course! But my teacher is very indulgent: myself. I never send myself to the little corner, not even when I have moments of depression and breaking down and real and true fear like I had two or three weeks ago. At Brett's request, I asked the administrative director of *L'Espresso* if I could return to Rome in October rather than in January. I was embarrassed but it went well. He spoke about it to V., who, after reacting to it suspiciously, said that "it certainly isn't my highest priority" and that he "has a lot of things to do." According to P., who knows him, it is a positive sign and will end up with him saying yes!! Another thing that worries me is that Brett maintains that I should talk to Stefano, perhaps not during this visit but in August, even if now it is no longer hideable and he is big enough and unspoken secrets fester. I know that he is right but I hate to see Stefano suffer and not be able in the least to express it. We'll see. We still have many months to think about it.

Dear sister, I've obsessed over my problems but you mustn't think that I am not well. On the contrary, this is a good period, and I am generally serene from morning till night. I would like, as always, to use my time better, but this is an old story. Write me soon. A big hug. Gio.

Sag Harbor (NY), Sunday, May 26, 1991

Dear Donatella,

Thank you so much for the octagonal book and your letter. I liked almost all of the stories and I was evidently inspired by them to want to write for children, so I tried to write a short story about a little boy whose mother makes buildings and he participates in the construction of a skyscraper.

We are spending a wonderful Memorial Day weekend (from Thursday evening until Monday afternoon) at Fran and Howard Kiernan's house. Sam is here too. Zach is having a great time. Howard works in the garden and Zach helps him like a busy beaver. The pool is not ready yet, so we bought a little plastic pool about two meters in diameter.

James Revson is in the area too, and I am a little nervous about the possibility of accidentally running into him. He never changed his mind about not seeing me or having any contact with me. On his last birthday in January, I sent him a card, but he never acknowledged it. He was in the hospital recently, and Sam asked him if he wanted me to come to see him, and he said no with a certain vehemence. Apparently, he has lost about thirty pounds and doesn't look well at all.

I have lost about thirteen pounds myself, which, in proportion to James, is more or less the same, and I don't look terrific either on some days. I hope that everything will go well on our wedding day because sometimes I have a gray and worn face that is impossible not to notice.

This, and the fact that my medications are increasing and that I sleep about ten hours a night with a two-hour nap, as well as other psychological factors that are a little more difficult to define, has strengthened my resolution to talk to Stefano. Not now, since he will be here for only a week and I want him to be only joyful, but in August when we're together for an entire month on Fire Island, a beautiful and almost magical place where I think the time will be right. I am very afraid of this conversation. The two possible outcomes are equally difficult for me: one, that he'll cry; or, even worse, two, that he'll feign indifference.

With some pressuring from Brett, I asked the director of *L'Espresso* if I could return to Rome in October rather than January. I haven't gotten his answer yet, but I don't see why he should say no. As far as Christmas, I would be glad to spend it with you in Milan but, obviously, I can't be sure that I'll be able to.

[...]My world is narrowing greatly, but I don't regret my old follies. [...] A big hug, Gio.

9

June 1, 1991

Dear Gio,

We're getting married. Soon. Between now and the day that "soon" becomes "now" (I can't wait!) there are countless details to attend to if we're to be able to sit back after the event and feel that our loved ones have the kind of glow about it—and us—that our irrepressible egos require. The yarmulkes, engraving the rings, the kiddush cup and tallis, new shoes for Zach, a suit for Stefano, how we are going to keep sixty bottles of liquor properly chilled, commandeering a roach exodus from the apartment, restoring our carpet to virgin whiteness, and on and on and on in precisely the way we'd set out to avoid. These details, however, have to do with the wedding only, and they mustn't divert us from the fact of our marriage, which is so much more than these details or even the ritual, the public acknowledgment, the celebration. It is our seal, our commitment, our official giving up a part of the "I" in order to meld it into the "We," which in our case is comprised of four, not the traditional two. We must not lose sight of that and the responsibility that the "We" carries.

Responsibility of the "We." It has its practical facets, like keeping the medicine cabinet closed to assure the well-being of Zach; it has its subtler, softer facets, like a hug out of the blue or lips pressed against the other's elbow at an unexpected 2 a.m. in an act of willed expression and not simply an accidental wisp of contact in mid-dream; and it has its larger, more looming facets, like daring to think ahead or choosing to put aside one's interests for the greater well-being of the relationship/family. Sometimes (rarely, thank God) the two are at odds. One must knowingly submit to individual pain for the greater well-being of the whole. Greater well-being must prevail in these rare instances. That's the substance of marriage: maturity, responsibility to the relationship.

Giovanni, my love, before we move to Rome, I ask you to undergo one of these rare instances. You must do several things to which you are entirely unaccustomed and which may cause you discomfort and perhaps some pain. I've spoken to you about them before. Nothing happened. I mention them again but no more. And I cannot allow Zach and me to move to Rome unless you show us that you have the well-being of all of us in mind and in your actions. You must prepare a will. You must find out about the health benefits you are entitled to, particularly long-term disability. This move is about and for all of us, but it pulls from us in very different ways. For you, it is a moving back to what is known and to many people who love you. For Zach and me, it is moving away from so much that is known and upon which our security is built. I am moving for the benefit of the entire family. You must show us that you have all of us in mind as well.

Responsibility to the relationship, the family. Please. I love you. Brett.

Silvia, Stefano, and Giovanni's father, Francesco, arrived in New York individually, beginning about one week before the wedding. Giovanni's sisters couldn't attend. Giovanni had decided that his parents, who had been divorced for almost twenty years and separated for thirty, were not going to stay in our apartment, and they settled into the one-bedroom apartment, about ten blocks away, of a friend of ours who was out of town. Francesco was staying for three weeks, and he and I spent most of our time together talking about Giovanni's health. Francesco had wanted to visit Giovanni's doctor, but Giovanni adamantly (to me) refused. I remember how resistant Giovanni had been to my going to his doctor for consultations. He had admitted to me that restricting the doctor-patient relationship to the two of them helped him to feel that the illness could be kept small, that the more people who entered into this compact, the more room the illness had to maneuver. I shared this construct of his when Francesco asked, and we denied him permission to visit the doctor, and I became to Francesco what Giovanni's doctor was for me: a thorough, dispassionate chronicler and statistician of the past and the present, completely reticent and noncommittal about the future.

Stefano was diverted from the deterioration of Giovanni's health by accompanying Silvia and me through the final swell of wedding details, which included buying him his first jacket and tie, and by spending time at the house of his friend Matthew. Giovanni was working only sporadically, but we decided to let Stefano assume that his father was working every day, rather than let him witness Giovanni continually lying on the sofa reading or sleeping.

My parents arrived June 23, the morning of the wedding.

My sisters couldn't attend. Silvia and Francesco came to the apartment at noon. I prepared pasta and salad for lunch, after which Giovanni, who had awakened at 10, went to take a nap while the remaining seven of us visited in the living room and awaited the caterers. I woke Giovanni up one hour later, and at that moment, all my anxiety vanished. I realized that its wellspring was about the state of Giovanni's health immediately preceding the wedding and had nothing to do with the details of the event: Giovanni had had eleven hours of sleep plus a one-hour nap immediately before the wedding. He would make it! From that point on, the roles were reversed. I was unflinchingly calm and completely absorbed by the rabbi's words and our vows; Giovanni, who, as he himself often confessed, had exhibitionist tendencies that enabled him to thrive in the spotlight, was a bundle of nerves hovering somewhere above, but not in, the ceremony. Zach and Stefano were the ring bearers, although Zach refused to remain under the huppah for more than two seconds and, in fact, provided a comic counterpoint by scrambling around the sanctuary trying his adorable best to veer the attention toward him. Toward the end of the ceremony, I had to pick him up and nestle him on my shoulder under the tallis that Giovanni and I shared.

It was over. The leap of my life—or was it out of my life?—had been taken. We were married. The reception was a joyful unwinding into the arms and best wishes of about seventy friends and family members. At some point, Giovanni stole away to the bedroom and took a second nap, and at 6:30, we slipped into a taxi and headed uptown where we were spending our one-night honeymoon at the Hotel Carlyle. To my surprise, Giovanni took a third nap upon our arrival. I went to the hotel bar and had a few drinks, then went outside and sat on the steps of the Metropolitan Museum. The ceremony, the reception, the momentary respite had transported me out of my incessant anguish. Now, peering across Fifth Avenue, I was back in New York, in my life, alone again. A few blocks away lay my spouse of five hours, impotent, invalid, supine for the third time. We would not be whisking off to the Caribbean for a week of lambent passion. We would never be whisking off to the Caribbean, nor would we ever have a night of passion again. The day had been so full; the future felt so bereft. I cried, took a deep breath, and stepped into the future. Giovanni was still asleep when I entered our hotel room. I woke him up, we ordered dinner in our room, and, afterward, made love. Despite his physical inabilities, Giovanni willed, for the final time, a kind of passion, of which I could feel the mental effort if not the sensual reward. The next morning, we had a late breakfast in bed, then ambled our way through Central Park, making frequent rest stops and, finally, reaching the west side, hailed a taxi home.

Three weeks later, Giovanni left for Italy. It was a trip that had prevailed in spite of a few arguments. The purpose of the visit, as Giovanni had led me to believe, was to sign papers for the divorce proceedings that Giovanni and his wife, from whom he'd been separated for more than a decade, had begun on Giovanni's last visit to Italy. I didn't understand why the papers couldn't wait until we arrived in Italy three months later. If Giovanni and his estranged wife had waited ten years to begin divorce proceedings, what were another three months, after all? Giovanni added to this rationale the fact that he wanted to see Stefano. I pointed out that Stefano had been with us only three weeks before and that he would be joining us in less than two weeks for a month on Fire Island and then we'd all be in Rome together only one month after that. Besides, I'd added, he was going to miss both Zach's and my birthdays, for which I was planning a big party, and, most importantly, I felt that he was in no condition to travel. Giovanni maintained an obstinacy about this trip that was anomalous to the point of being suspect.

On the morning of his departure, James Revson died. It had been written up in the *New York Times*, which I'd read early that morning at the gas station while Zach, aided by the Pakistani attendant, was tinkering with his tricycle. My initial reaction was to try to prevent Giovanni from reading the paper that day, and I considered not bringing the *Times* home with me. I couldn't bear the thought of Giovanni going off to Italy with such news festering in his brain and without a sufficient interval of myself to provide consolation. At the same time, I knew that keeping Giovanni away from the *Times* would be more difficult than getting Stefano into a shower.

When Zach and I returned home, I told Giovanni that James had died and then gave him the paper. He was silent, devastated, grieving. His willed impetus of gaiety was ebbing away. I knew what he was thinking: my fate has been sealed. My rage about his imprudent trip to Italy deflated. All I wanted was some time with him before he left to help close the wound. But this I was not going to have.

During my week alone with Zach, I decided to wean him completely from the bottle, which he was taking twice a day. I talked to him each day about his coming birthday and how, at the age of three, it would be nice to give his bottles to a baby who needed them. The day before his party—a maelstrom of twelve toddlers minimally supervised by parents who were only too pleased to have the wreckage taking place outside of their own home—Zach and I put his bottles into a box, wrapped the box in flowered paper and ribbons, and after the party, Zach proudly handed it to the infant daughter of my best friend. I had hidden one bottle in a kitchen cabinet just in case Zach's withdrawal proved too excruciating for him—or me—to withstand. Zach had one brief writhing-on-the-floor tantrum before bedtime and another the following morning. Then it was over. However, to this day, at the age of four, he will not drink milk. He is angry at milk since it no longer comes in its desired receptacle. Perhaps I should have waited. Traveling was accessory-free for two months; in mid-September, props began to appear again, this time for Giovanni.

On the day of his return, Giovanni told me the real reason for his trip to Italy. He had been asked to host a week-long radio show in Rome in which listeners called in with questions and commentary about politics, and Giovanni was to be both punter and pundit. Giovanni's passion was politics, second only to his love of being in the public eye. The combination was irresistible. However, the program was to be broadcast live each morning at 7:00, and Giovanni was afraid that if he had told me beforehand, particularly about the ungodly hours, I would have refused to let him go. A wave of incredulity and hurt came over me. How little he knows me, I thought. And yet at the same time, I was disturbed by what his perceptions of me must be—and, more importantly, how I actually contributed to those perceptions—if he thought I would react in that way. I told him, "Actually, that's the sanest reason you've given for going to Italy. You would have had my blessing, and my relentless nagging to make sure to take care of yourself."

Two days after Giovanni's return, I received a phone call from Walnes, the first time I'd spoken to him in more than a year. He was calling to ask me if I could rummage through the boxes he had stored in my basement in Brooklyn to find three documents that he needed in order to try and obtain a resident visa for his mother, who was visiting him from Haiti. We spoke without any friction for almost a half hour, and I suggested that he join me in the rummage and afterward I would take him to lunch. "I would like that very much," he said, "but to be honest, given my physical condition, I can't really go out of the house." He then went on to explain that he'd been in and out of the hospital for the last four months with toxoplasmosis and pneumonia and was still recovering. He accepted my alternative that Zach and I come to visit him after we found the documents in the basement.

The encounter was wrenching. Walnes was lying on a sofa, barely able to move. He weighed no more than eighty-five pounds, his skin was mottled and leathern, his hair in filmy tufts, his eyes vacant and pained. His mother kept shuffling into the room trying to force-feed him. A few days after this visit, Walnes went back into the hospital. He died on July 29, 1991. His funeral was scheduled for the day of our move to Fire Island. I didn't go.

Giovanni didn't go to the funeral or to Fire Island on July 29. Although he wanted to help me move our belongings to the Island, Stefano was arriving from Italy the following day, and I persuaded Giovanni that it would be sheer foolishness for him to make the trek, only to have to return to New York the day after to pick Stefano up at the airport and then make the trek back to Fire Island again. Instead, I suggested that he remain behind and come to the island the day after Stefano arrived. That way, the house would be completely set up, and he could immediately fall into the relaxed pace that the month promised. I also took the opportunity at this moment to tell him that I'd asked Judith to come to the island every week during the two days that I had to work in New York so that she could help him with Zach and Stefano and with the general household chores like cooking and shopping. Giovanni took offense at my decision, feeling that for two days a week he could easily manage, but in the end, he agreed to try it for the first week. Judith continued to come to the island throughout the month.

I convinced him ... I persuaded him ... I refused to let him ... I nagged him ... the voice of reason forever lunging at the voice of denial ... or was it the voice of control merely trying to convince and persuade itself that it did have some control? that if Giovanni took just this one more nap, drank just this one more can of Sustecal, he would then stop getting weaker, losing weight, dying? In my many shrill and fitful moments with Giovanni when I would accuse him of not knowing how to take care of himself, of being too heedless before this monster illness, I was actually denouncing him for inadvertently reminding me, over and over again, how powerless I was. Nonetheless, my grip on his illness remained inviolate, and it wasn't until our last secret hope—Switzerland—was dashed that each of us let go of our respective and ever-chafing survival tactics, let our wills arrange themselves for defeat, and eased into a unified and gentle acceptance.

10

Seaview (Fire Island), August 4

Dear Emanuela,

I just finished reading *The Scarlet Letter* by Hawthorne. A story about sin, expiation, and redemption in Puritan New England of 1600-1700. It was written in an old style of English which made it a little difficult for me to read. Now I will tackle *Villette* by Charlotte Bronte and then maybe *War and Peace*. But I don't know if I will have the time and desire.

Right now, everyone is outside. I just woke up from a nap. The house is shady and cool, a pleasant little breeze runs through; everything is surrounded by pine trees, bushes, and other trees. It reminds me a bit of Montepilli but more closed in and worn. But the same type of bric-a-brac and everything of wood. Outside, there is a deck that allows one to be in communion with nature but privately. There are deer throughout the island that chew all the plants and are carriers of Lyme disease. So, they're talking about permitting hunting again like they did in 1988 when sixty deer were killed. Wouldn't it be enough just to sterilize them, I say.

The house is bigger than I remembered it from the

first visit in spring. There is an L-shaped, closed-in veranda. The living room is large, with a worn-out sofa and wicker armchairs and a table on which I am writing to you. The kitchen is average. Next to the bathroom is a tiny guest room. From the living room, a narrow stairway goes to the second floor where there are four bedrooms laid out strangely, each with a little sink. And there is a toilet, a little room with a tiny window that looks out on the tops of the trees. This is the place where we will relax and be well, each with the other? The ingredients are there, but it isn't only in our surroundings that we find quiet so much as, and above all, within us. And that's where things get more complicated. Brett, so much for change, is very tense and transmits his tension to Zach, who, not used to being with Brett so much, behaves badly. Stefano has his friend Matthew with him until August 12, and this is going very well. They returned just now. Matthew is doing his homework, and Stefano is absorbed in reading the rules of a game.

This morning, I spoke to him during a walk along the beach. As is his custom, he didn't react. When I asked him if he had any questions, he answered in a flat tone, "There's nothing to ask." To reassure him, I emphasized that Brett and Sam are negative and that I have the best treatment possible from both the domestic and the clinical points of view. "Nasino di topo!" Luckily, we have a month ahead of us during which time whatever doubts, anxieties, and questions he may have can come to the surface. There's also Brett and, a little later, Sam.

Now it is night. We were outside until just a short while ago, Brett and I playing Frisbee and Stefano and Matthew racquetball. Now, besides me, Zach also has diarrhea. I bought arsenicum and have been using it for two days. (I couldn't find the mineral salts.) Tonight, we went to a stupendous restaurant on the ocean, but I could have only soup a salad, and rice. Right now, it's raining and all the towels were left outside. Squic.

Tomorrow and the day after Brett won't be here; he's going to New York to work—I confess that I am not sad because there is less tension, but it is sad that I have to say this. (Anyway, tonight I want to sleep in Zach's room so that Brett can sleep uninterruptedly— he has to wake up at 5 a.m.)

Now that a series of decisions about our move has been made and things have been said, I feel a lot better. I can't wait to show Rome to Brett. He says that I won't have time, that I'll have to work and he'll be left alone all day with a three-year-old. He is very negative, unfortunately, and I don't know what to do to cheer him up a little. He is afraid, and, in fact, sure that we won't be able to find a big enough apartment. But this can be disproved quickly. And on and on. I think that he concentrates on these marginal things to hide his enormous anxiety, which he prefers not to talk about. [...]By the way, at least in the beginning, we could pile into via Mameli with you or else in some other temporary place (I don't want to even ask Mother if we could use her apartment).

I hope that all is going well, that your circle of [yoga] clients is growing, and that the week at Jesolo is instructive. A big hug, Gio.

Fire Island, Wednesday, August 21

Dearest Mammetta,

We had a big adventure: Hurricane Bob almost hit us. We had to evacuate in a pouring rain with water up to our knees to take the last ferry back to the mainland. It was also the day of the coup against Gorbachev, so it really felt like Armageddon, except both things ended with no great damage. Actually, I think that the outcome in the USSR is positive because they have now conquered their freedom, rather than having had it bestowed on them like before. The hurricane is having some lingering consequences: we still have no power. Brett hustled all day to get them to work on restoring electricity to our house. A few minutes ago, the electricity came back. Brett rushed to the washing machine and I to the TV to watch the news. But in no time, a big transformer blew with an ominous sound and we're in the dark again. It was quite cozy last night with only candles, and tonight we're having a fire whether the electricity comes back or not.

Poor Zach is very unhappy, eaten alive by the bugs. He scratches himself all the time, making things much worse. His face is all puffed up, his eyes are swollen, his left ear is twice as big as the right one. The itching is driving him crazy. We wiped him with all sorts of creams and repellents but to no avail. Finally, today, Brett found a combination of antihistamines and something you swallow, and it seems to be working. We're having a very busy social life. The first ten days, Matthew came, which was good for Stefano. Then Brett's sister, Barbara. Subsequently, Fabrizio for just two days. Barbara's daughter, Dana, age fourteen, stayed here for a week and it was a huge success. She and Stef hit it off famously. They moved in together in the guesthouse behind the deck from where they would emerge around midday with sleepy eyes. We didn't inquire about what went on, but I think it was all quite innocent, mostly endless games of Monopoly (a metaphor for the ancient game of seduction?). He was quite believable as a pursuer of a girl three years his senior (she will be fifteen before he is thirteen). He's big and mature and somewhat more sophisticated than her (although they could both behave delightfully childlike). It was a pleasure having her here.

Now (Thursday the 22nd) Sam and Jimmy, who have been staying here for the past week, are getting ready to leave. Sam was a pillar of strength during the hurricane, and it was he who made the decision to evacuate while I was wringing my hands, not quite able to decide the best course. Brett was in New York and I'm afraid I have grown used to deferring to him. Later it turned out that we could in fact have stayed but why take a chance, especially with young children?

I'm listening to Dvorak in the golden afternoon. Everybody is at the beach, but I was too weak to go. Sam and Jimmy are good with Zach. Brett can use all the help he can get with this handful of a child because, unfortunately, I'm quite useless. What pleases me the most is that Stefano is very attentive and tender with Zach and doesn't need to be asked to step in. He's growing fast, maybe too fast, but it can't be avoided. I finally spoke with him about my condition, but between my being obscure and my not using the "A" word, he had not quite understood what it was about. A few days later, Brett did explain it without reticence and also gave him the chance to ask questions and express feelings. I'm so glad to have him at my side.

My health, as you may have gathered, is not great. I had a blessed ten days without fever and I enjoyed them to the fullest, but then the fever came back with a vengeance. Last night at midnight, I had 100.5 and took two Tylenol. Two hours later, I was burning with 100.9. Diarrhea is also rampant, very liquid, and happens many times a day. It weakens me a great deal. I can't fully participate in the joyous and messy life of this household. I sit back, content to watch and exchange a smile, a bit of conversation, a squeeze. It's not nearly enough for Brett, who, especially when I give him a rough night with my insomnia, becomes a little snappy. Everything is exacerbated by the mosquitos that pick on little defenseless Zach. His face is disfigured, all puffed up and marked, one ear is—but I'm realizing now that this was already in the beginning of the letter. I'm repeating myself, better to conclude.

I count on you to start looking for an apartment for me in September. It should definitely be a three-bedroom or, if the kitchen is large and can be used as a dining-living room, a two-bedroom. Brett fears that we'll end up in a hole in the periphery and I can't convince him it won't happen. He's so Russian (I'm reading *War and Peace*!!!)

OK, Mammetta, it's time for me to go to the beach (it's 4:30 and the sun doesn't harm) and spend some time with my guys. Lots and lots of love, Gio.

With the exception of a one-hour, late-afternoon visit to the beach, Giovanni rarely left the house on Fire Island. Toward the second half of the month, he was unable to walk more than two blocks without becoming entirely breathless and exhausted. Moreover, his diarrhea had become uncontrollable, sometimes as often as fifteen times a day, and nightly fevers were as reliable as the sound of the waves through our bedroom window. Although it was a sweltering August, Giovanni was always cold.

My days passed in much the same way as my weekends in New York. Each morning when Zach woke up, we'd quickly slip out to the village, Zach eating his breakfast in the little red wagon I used to cart the groceries home and I sipping my coffee. We'd spend one or two hours at the playground, then do the grocery shopping for the day, and return home, usually to find Stefano still bivouacked in the small guesthouse and Giovanni seated at the living room table, writing or reading. After breakfast, I'd take the children to the beach where they'd spend the entire afternoon; I'd return at lunchtime to pack a lunch to bring to the beach and to prepare something for Giovanni. At about 4:30, Giovanni would join us at the beach, shrouded in shirts and towels and a broad-brimmed hat. We'd return home at around 6:00, and I'd make dinner, shortly after which Giovanni and Zach would go to bed. I was also thoroughly exhausted well before the end of each day and usually sat on the beach at night for an hour or two of lamentation and renewal, with or without Stefano, before collapsing into bed. In the frail husk of Giovanni's body, the same alert and appetitive mind lived, and I couldn't believe that this mental energy couldn't somehow find a way into its corporeal shell. Panic and fury are so interchangeable for me as to seem like one emotion, and each day I was growing more and more furious.

One week after our return from Fire Island, I made Giovanni go into the hospital. It was clear that every day he was growing frailer, and my obsessive care and myriad home remedies were not sustaining him. His doctor was able to procure him a bed in the AIDS ward of St. Luke's-Roosevelt

Hospital where the facilities resemble an adult camp: shows, socials, lectures and seminars, a lounge/library with a television and piano. Although Giovanni was horrified that he was going into the hospital, the moment he settled into his bed he relaxed and, in fact, seemed more at ease than when he was at home. He was able to sleep and read as he pleased without a sense of guilt over not participating in family life, and the highlight of his days came when the menu arrived in the morning, and he was able to make his selections for the three meals of the day. At first, he had refused to have visitors but soon consented to having one or two a day. He was always tired and, in addition, felt uncomfortable having his friends see him hooked up to the 24-hour-a-day I/V of nutrients that was the principal component of his treatment. Propped up on his pillows, surrounded by periodicals and books, and in a setting that required nothing of him but rest, he told me he felt almost regal.

Giovanni refused to leave his room. He didn't want to see the other patients. Walking down the corridors and peering irresistibly into each room would have been like walking down a hall of mirrors, and once again, remaining in his bed enabled him to feel that the illness was small, contained, excluded from the portentous statistics.

I was relieved as well. Back on Horatio Street, it felt as if sanctions had been lifted. The apartment was Zach's playground once more, mornings could be delightfully clamorous, and Daddy was there for him 100 percent. The perpetual clashes of needs had been physically separated.

On one of my visits to the hospital, Giovanni asked me to sit on the bed and take his hand. "I want you to know that however you feel the need to satisfy your sexual needs, you have my blessing." This roundabout allusion of his, such a rarity, to a tangible consequence of his illness so terrified me that my rage immediately intervened. "I don't need you to grant me permission to be unfaithful!" Fortunately, I was able to keep the comment to myself, and to Giovanni I said nothing, only smiled. It wasn't until I was taking the subway home that I realized how difficult it must have been for him to say that to me, how much fragile hope he had had to forfeit in order to let me know how much he loved me and wanted my needs taken care of, even if it meant my satisfying them elsewhere. For so long, I'd been accosting Giovanni about slighting his illness and, in so doing, inadvertently increasing the dosage of tumult it injected into all our lives. Finally, when a moment of acknowledgment came, it took away from me precisely what I'd thought it would fortify: my strength. I was reminded once more that I needed Giovanni's hope and denial, however they were fashioned, in order to be strong, just as he needed my vigilance and competence. There was almost a perfect symmetry in operation, a tacit allegiance between these opponents.

New York, September 13, 1991

Dear Donatella,

Thank you for your letter. You are one of the few people who maintains a correspondence. It is sad that this art is dying. Even people who write for a living don't write back to me. The cursed telephone.

Today I had a colonoscopy and various biopsies of my stomach. They gave me Demerol and I was really out of it. It was very pleasant. Not that I would want to try it again. They are looking to discover the causes of my diarrhea with the hope of stopping it or at least curbing it. Things are not going well, and I have the impression that Babbo isn't sufficiently aware of what is going on. Maybe you could help him to prepare himself. However, I imagine that it is difficult for you as well. My weight has dropped a lot again, and I am beginning to have "that look." Brett is very brave and very good through all of this, but sometimes he can't take it. So, he started to go to two support groups: one for people who are very close to someone who is sick (not necessarily with AIDS; one woman has a husband with Parkinson's), and another for "codependents." This concept is very a la mode here. It's difficult to explain, but I would say without a doubt that for many years you were this way with respect to Babbo: doing everything FOR the person and in place of the person, then feeling resentment about it, and looking to control the activities and even feelings of the person. This is the portrait of Brett with regard to us. You'll say to me: "But I thought that this was what being good meant!" And it is, but there are darker sides. Americans "medicalize" too much, but I am convinced that this is a real personality disturbance. Also because it repeats itself.

On Sunday the 13th, my colleague Andrea Visconti is giving us an "arrivederci party" (better than "farewell," which is too final), and for the first time in five years there will be a substantial gathering of select Italian colleagues—whom I have seen very little of—and my (and Brett's) American friends. A big hug, Gio.

In addition to the I/V of nutrients, Giovanni had a battery of blood tests as well as the colonoscopy, from which came the diagnosis: cytomegalovirus (CMV) cohabitating with the parasite cryptosporidium. CMV is a bona fide opportunistic infection that usually strikes either the brain, resulting in dementia, or the eyes, resulting in blindness. In Giovanni's case, the CMV and the parasite were only in his colon. The doctors assured us that the former could be eliminated and the latter controlled with appropriate medications. This would mean that the diarrhea would go away, the energy would come back, the weight would be restored. In other words, another episode, another symptom-as-the-illness that would pass, this time, however, with a significant shift in the semantic nuance: from a clinical point of view, Giovanni was no longer simply HIV positive. He had AIDS.

In addition to Beedie, Giovanni would now have another constant companion: a catheter. Rather than injecting a needle into his vein every day, a port was to be surgically implanted in his stomach with an internal catheter going up his chest to his collarbone which would permit the daily one-hour infusions of DHPG, the medication that would eliminate the CMV but only if used for life. Giovanni was released from the hospital two days after the surgery. On the morning of his release, I arrived at the hospital with a present for him, for us: a cocoa-colored leather-and-metal wheelchair. As memorabilia, Giovanni took home with him the plastic portable urinal so that he wouldn't have to get out of bed five to ten times a night to urinate. On the advice of the doctor, when we arrived home, we threw out the scale. "Do not obsess over his weight," he had told us.

For the first week after Giovanni returned home, a nurse came to the house each morning after I took Zach to school to teach me how to set up and administer the I/V for which there were more than twenty-five pieces. The most trying part was inserting the butterfly needle into the port, which had to first penetrate Giovanni's flesh. Attached to the needle was a slender plastic tube, about three inches long, which dangled from Giovanni's stomach. At the end of this tube was a rubber cap, and it was into this rubber cap that the I/V needle itself was placed. Once inserted, the butterfly needle could be kept in the port for three days as long as it was covered securely with a transparent I/V dressing to minimize the chance of infection when Giovanni took showers.

The entire intravenous procedure took almost two hours a day. We decided to perform it at night after Zach went to sleep. I would prepare the refrigerated DHPG solution and assemble the I/V in the kitchen while Giovanni was getting ready for bed and would start the infusion when he was tucked in. "Don't go," he'd say to me when I'd finished, and I'd sit with him and talk or massage him until he fell asleep, usually within twenty minutes. I'd retreat to the living room, and every fifteen minutes tiptoe back into the bedroom and hold a match under the infusion, which was suspended upside down from a hanger that was hooked to a lamp on the night table (we hadn't yet graduated to a pole), to see whether it was dripping at the proper rate: one drop every two seconds. By the time the infusion had finished and I had disconnected the tubing and accessories and separated all the disposable parts—those through which medication had flowed, or had possibly come in contact with bodily fluid, had to be discarded in a special red plastic canister that was picked up weekly by the medical supply company; the rest could be tossed in the "normal" garbage—it was 11:00, my desired bedtime.

For life.

11

The October 3 target date for our move to Rome was pushed back because Flaminia and her boyfriend Andrea chose to visit us for three weeks at the end of September, and Giovanni had been encouraging his sister to visit New York ever since he'd arrived. The revised date, October 15, was set back again because a good friend of mine in Boston was getting married on the 19th and I wanted to attend the wedding. (As it turned out, I didn't go.) The third and final date was set: October 24. I quit my job soon after Giovanni's release from the hospital, feeling that he was homebound and required the equivalent of a nurse, if not by his side, at least in the house. Also, it was time to figure out how to get our household across the Atlantic.

The logistics were overwhelming. First, there was Brooklyn. My personal possessions stored in Brooklyn had to be re-stored at my parents' house or discarded. Moreover, Walnes's effects had to be sorted through. I loathed the idea of spending an afternoon in my basement with Walnes's mother, whom I'd never met, who spoke only Creole and didn't know that Walnes was gay, let alone that he'd died of AIDS, examining each and every remnant of paper and clothing. I called a mutual friend of Walnes's and his mother's who spoke English to arrange for a suitable time. He said to me, "Marie wants to know if it is safe to touch Walnes's clothing."

As it turned out, Walnes's mother did not try to pollinate

each and every personal effect with her private melancholy. Rather, she callously handled the items, making snap decisions about their fate (usually to throw them into the garbage) as if they'd been accomplices in Walnes's death. At the end of three days, the basement was empty, with the exception of the items for the movers to pack and drive to Philadelphia.

Then there was Manhattan. Three sorts were involved. I was taking nothing of mine to Rome except clothes and toys for Zach, whatever could fit into three suitcases and one trunk. I knew what was going to happen in Rome, and I had my own intuitive idea of when but what I didn't know was whether I'd continue on in Rome once the thing had happened. When the movers arrived to prepare an estimate, Giovanni and I escorted them through the apartment. As they pointed to each object, I indicated "Philadelphia," "Rome," or "Staying here." Giovanni was aghast at the number of times I said "Philadelphia." "Why aren't you taking that picture? You love it so much ... Why are you leaving that chair? Why can't we take your piano? Why aren't you taking ANYTHING?" I had told Giovanni why before, but now that the verdict was being reiterated throughout the house and committed to the inventory sheets, Giovanni was stunned.

"Do I really have to explain it to you again? I don't have the patience or the peace of mind to be soft about it. It might be better for you to try to remember the reason yourself."

"No, tell me," he urged.

"Because you're going to die in Rome, and I don't know if I'll want, or be in a position, to stay. And the last thing I'll want to have to deal with is spending the time and another $10,000 to move back everything that was moved over."

"Oh." Sad, wet puppy dog expression pleading with me to find a way to not allow it to be so.

In a softer tone: "I'm sorry, but one day you're not going to be here, and Zach and Stef and I will still be here, having to deal with the things that don't go away because you have and having to deal with them through an abysmal sense of loss. I'm trying in advance to not let things fall apart when the day comes for things to fall apart. Call it desperate sanity-grabbing. I try to keep your death a secret from you, but sometimes you won't let me. I'm sorry."

New York, September 15, 1991

Dear Kathy,

Thank you for your kind words. I also feel a bond of sorts with you, through Sam.

On this side of the continent, we are getting ready for the move. Exciting and scary. Many things to decide and to take care of, many stops—Manhattan, Brooklyn, Philadelphia. Brett is already very tired and I'm afraid the actual move might be too much for him. I feel like I'm floating in the air. I'm shrinking, both physically (I'm down to 107 pounds) and metaphorically. I can participate in the life around me less and less, and I don't really want to. I'm beginning to understand how very old people must feel. It's a way of letting go of worldly matters. Unfortunately, those "matters" also include people with their feelings. I love Brett more every day. I feel I haven't finished my job with Stefano. And I really wish I had a chance to become part of Zach's life. That's the worst part, letting go of people you love. Today I was at a picnic in the park with my guys, and that feeling was so overwhelming that I lay down and . . . in a minute I was asleep! I always have that escape, although my sleep is more and more disturbed.

I hope everything is fine with you. Actually, we have this mad dream of moving one day to Berkeley.

Who knows? Maybe one day we'll be neighbors. Give my best to Bob. A big hug, Giovanni.

Silvia brought us the welcome news that she had found an apartment for us that met all of our requirements as well as our desires: in Trastevere where both she and Manu had their apartments, three bedrooms (one for Zach, one for Stefano, one for Giovanni and me), a terrace, and on the first floor. (We had set a limit for nonelevator buildings of eighteen steps from sidewalk to apartment. This one had twelve.) The price was outrageous and, on paper, made a mockery out of our budget, but I was so tired of organizing and reorganizing and arguing and forever floating in a limbo of speculation and contingency planning—all of which was increasingly seeming so desperately urgent and so utterly pointless at the same time—that I deferred to Giovanni. The assurance that we would have a permanent place to live within a week of our arrival was worth it, and, besides, I knew that our life was going to be confined to the house, which made its dimensions and amenities even more important. In the course of my conversation with Silvia about the apartment, and against Giovanni's wishes, I told her about the wheelchair.

Flaminia and Andrea arrived at the end of September and stayed with us for three weeks. Zach and I had now met and spent a good deal of time with the Forti family. Rome would be less alien to me now, and I was grateful that we had established strong links to those who were to become the principal figures in our life.

The week before the move was designated "Doctors' Week." I doubled up on my therapy sessions, took Zach to the dentist for his first visit, and took myself to the dentist for the first time in two years. I also brought our two cats, who were moving with us, to the veterinarian to obtain the required vaccinations and certificates of health. The younger cat, who was sixteen, had a tumor and was put to sleep. The older cat, who was eighteen, was showing signs of kidney failure, but we decided to bring her. My main concern was transporting enough supplies for Giovanni's medical care so that we wouldn't have to worry about them as soon as we deplaned. I was told by the Italian Consulate that no prescription drugs were permitted in the country, that a letter from a doctor could perhaps help, but there was no guarantee since it was entirely at the discretion of the individual customs officer through whom we would pass. Nevertheless, I spent six hours one afternoon compiling an inventory of each and every medication and accessory Giovanni was using (the list totaled more than fifty items) and calculating how many of each would be necessary to last us for six weeks. When the order arrived, Flaminia and Andrea each cached a four-day supply, the size of two large shoeboxes, in their luggage as a kind of emergency stock in the event our mother lode didn't get through customs. The remaining five-week supply went into a box about the size of a refrigerator minus the freezer compartment. This was to go on the plane with us, along with the cat kennel, the wheelchair, Zach's car seat, five suitcases, and a family-size picnic cooler in which I had to put one of Giovanni's medications that required refrigeration. The total cost of the supplies to last us six weeks, provided they got through customs: $33,000.

The final doctor visit in New York was to Giovanni's doctor, who provided us with the prescriptions, the letter for customs, and a copy of Giovanni's medical records. When Giovanni went to the reception area to pay the bill, I lingered in the doctor's office until Giovanni was out of sight. "I won't hold you to your prediction, but given our situation, I would like to know how long you think Giovanni has," I said. His reply: "Less than a year." "I give it about six months," I said. "You may be right," he said.

Giovanni's medical records had to be faxed to Switzerland, along with an application for admittance to the clinic. The acknowledgment letter that was faxed to us the following day informed us that the clinic would be closed from October through January since the facilities were being expanded and, most likely, relocated. When I called my contact, a Greek who was living in Boston and worked as a kind of administrator/liaison for the doctor, he told me that he was not permitted to disclose the name of the country where the new clinic would be opened. He also said there was a long waiting list, but that Giovanni would be admitted within the first few weeks of the clinic reopening, probably in late January or early February. Four months away.

The one and one-half months that we had in New York from the time Giovanni left the hospital until we moved to Rome were relatively stable ones in terms of Giovanni's health. His weight—about 105 pounds—held its own, the diarrhea was reduced to four or five times a day, nightly fevers could be counted upon. In the pockets of time between his two or three one- to two-hour naps, we made excursions with the help of the wheelchair. At first, Giovanni was reluctant to use the wheelchair in the immediate neighborhood, but soon yielded to its promise of longer outings and greater mobility. The wheelchair enabled us to go on frequent outings, during which I often wondered what configuration was being contrived behind the eyes of the people who stared at these two men and a baby and a wheelchair strolling down the sidewalks of the Village.

In a perverse but crucial way, the wheelchair restored the intimacy between Zach and Giovanni that had begun a year before and had been so quickly obviated, for now Zach was contentedly spending one or two hours each day on Giovanni's lap. In a similar crucial perversity, Giovanni's nightly intravenous infusions became our new form of intimacy: alone, in our room, at night, concentrated, quietly performing a delicate act in which fluids penetrated the body of one through the actions of another. Clinical erotica.

Three days before our departure date, the movers packed up everything that was to be put in storage at my parents' house. The following day, the van was loaded up with the one hundred boxes, made a stop in Brooklyn for the remaining items, and headed for Philadelphia. I accompanied the van; Zach stayed with Judith until I returned home that evening. The next morning, the movers returned to pack and load everything that was being shipped to Italy. By the end of that day, our apartment contained one sofa, one table, one fan, one palm tree, one yucca tree—all being left behind—and the things we were taking with us. We spent the night at a guesthouse a few blocks away and had dinner with Sam and Jimmy in a nearby restaurant.

Everything went smoothly, yet nothing seemed smooth. I lay awake that night, despite the Valium I'd taken (I'd begged my doctor for a two-week prescription after explaining the circumstances and adding that I'd never taken sedatives before), trying to squeeze these immensities of change into something that felt more in the daily course of things. After fourteen years—my entire adult life—I was leaving New York with my son (he alone an immensity of change by which I was still throttled) and a man who would soon be dead to a country I'd visited once behind the windows of a tour bus twenty years ago in which a language was spoken that was music to the ears and babble to the brain and everything and everyone that was in my exterior life that comfortably and with a soothing predictability pushed me from one minute into the next wouldn't be there starting tomorrow, and I'd be on terra incognita with a three-year-old and a terminally ill (but WHEN Goddamit it!) man, fending for them and for myself, and the months of organizing and preparing are over, and what can possibly fill the void besides its rightful tenant sheer terror and grief. I'm so tired, so unbearably tired, but I can't sleep because everything that isn't a marvel in my life, everything that is calm and steady and just there building and resuscitating and replenishing me without my scarcely having to think about it will no longer be there and I'll have only the marvels and newnesses and sources of constant awe and breathtaking concern, read Zach=Life, Giovanni=Death, untethered from my personal-safe-known vortex. Yes, this is my Brett-wild apogee.

12

Across the street from Manu's apartment are a series of steep pedestrian ramps that traverse the serpentine via Garibaldi three times, like the line through a dollar sign. They are overhung by bougainvillea, jacaranda, and other sheltering foliage so that during the ascent the air is dark, dank, and has a fecund interior aroma in which the city smells and noises are absorbed. At the top of the third chaparral is an esplanade, from which the cityscape of Rome can be seen in full panorama. It was here that Zach and I had our first vista of the city, as soon as we'd deposited our things in Manu's apartment where we were staying for the first week until our apartment was ready on November 1. Giovanni had made a beeline for the bedroom. Looking out over this new old world as Manu identified with pointed finger and soft husky voice the numerous edifices, ruins, domes, and other landmarks about which Giovanni had frequently said to me over the months, "I can't wait to take you to...," I knew that whatever sightseeing I managed to accomplish would be alone or, in any event, without Giovanni, and that, in all probability, a lot of my sightseeing had just taken place. Strangely, as extraordinarily beautiful as the vista was, my interest in exploring its historical and artistic particulars was only half-aroused. What was fully wakened was its opposite: how to negotiate it, domesticate it so that it would feel ordinary. I didn't want so much to feel exalted by the city as at home in it. "Where's the pharmacy?" pressed more forcefully upon me than "Where are the Caravaggios?"

By the end of the first day, virtually the entire family—Stefano, Giovanna, Flaminia, Silvia, Manu's two children—had paid a visit. Only Francesco, who had recently moved to Milan, couldn't be with us. Giovanni held court on the sofa. The proximity and solidarity of the family was enviable. I hoped that Zach and I would be able to enter its warm embrace in our own right, as much for a sense of a nuclear family as for the day-to-day assistance I could use.

"Before and after administering the DHPG, the port and catheter have to be flushed out with saline solution, and, as the last step, with heparin, an anti-clotting solution. Just remember SASH: Saline, Administration, Saline, Heparin. The saline solution is in these two vials with the pink tops. The syringes to be used are the thinnish ones, here. The needles that go on the syringes are enclosed in the pink case. Remember, pink with pink. The heparin is in the vial with the white cap. It uses the same syringe, but the needle is the one in the red case. It is a smaller needle. The neupogen, which is injected into Giovanni's thigh every day, alternating thighs, is kept in the refrigerator. It's already prepared, and the syringe already has the needle on it. It's the super-thin one. The neupogen raises the white cell count, which the DHPG has a nasty habit of lowering . . ." And so my lesson went the following evening after supper. Silvia and Manu were sitting around the dining room table where the smorgasbord of medical supplies had been laid out. The plan was to walk them through the administration of Giovanni's intravenous medications so that I wouldn't have a monopoly on this aspect of his care. From the look on Silvia's face as I proceeded with the lesson, I knew there was going to be at least one dropout, and I suddenly recalled my childhood Erector set booklet, filled with pictures of Ferris wheels and skyscrapers and cranes that could be constructed, and how as soon as I enthusiastically turned to the instructions, I became paralyzed. I couldn't bring myself to calmly walk through the sequence of the construction process. Instead, the entire process leapt at me in one giant complexity, for which my father always came to the rescue, constructing without instructing since I always disappeared until the project was complete. And so it was with Manu and Silvia. History repeated itself. Within two days I was a teacher without pupils.

Despite the persistently gray and damp weather, characteristic of Roman winters, Zach and I spent much of our time outdoors. One more tier up from the esplanade was a vast park, the Gianicolo, and in the neighborhood itself were a number of piazzas that we frequented. My bronchitis, which had begun two weeks before our move, was not getting any better. I certainly wasn't nursing it, and in retrospect, I think that the child in me wanted to become confined to bed in order to demonstrate to my small world how indispensable I was. On one afternoon, we went on our first brief sightseeing tour to the nearby Isola Tiberina with Giovanni in the wheelchair, Zach in his lap, and Stefano and I taking turns pushing the chair over the virtually sidewalk-less streets. By the time we returned home, I had blisters on my inner thumbs caused by the constant pressure I had to apply while steering the wheelchair in order to prevent it from careening into traffic as it bounced and bumped its way over each cobblestone. Giovanni actually complained of nausea from the bumps, saying it felt like air turbulence. The rest of the time during that week he spent in the apartment, either napping or receiving visitors.

The weekend before we moved into our apartment, Manu, her friend Rita, Giovanni, Stefano, Zach, and I went to the family's country home, Porvietoli, just outside of Grosseto in Tuscany. Giovanni remained close to the fireplace, the only source of heat, and the rest of us languished outdoors. Manu forced me to take it easy, to take naps, to sleep late; she even performed reiki on me several times in order to try to ease my bronchitis. But my coughing episodes were so severe that I tore some ligaments and had to huddle in a corner, almost vomiting, until the coughs subsided. Zach was tired out soon after dinner, and I was able to relax for a few hours at night after I'd put him to bed and given Giovanni his infusion, which Stefano witnessed for the first time. On the first evening, there were screams from our bedroom. Zach, who was accustomed to sleeping with his Donald Duck night light, awoke to find himself in darkness. "Daddy!" he was crying, "I can't see. My eyes fell out!"

"Well, how did you like Porvietoli?" Giovanni asked me on the drive back to Manu's.

"Lovely. What a wonderful place to be able to go to."

"Yes. But promise me one thing. Let's not go back until the weather is a little warmer. I can no longer take the cold."

We never made it back.

Rome, Tuesday, November 6

Dearest Sam,

You won't believe me when I tell you that this is the first time that I have time and am feeling well enough to write to you, but it's the truth. The other day I spent several hours alone listening to music and reading, but I was too exhausted to do anything. I had a few bad days, absolutely miserable and breathless. But my mood is unflagging. Today I'm feeling much better. I'm at Manu's, waiting for the repairmen to come and fix the washing machine: while we were staying here, Zach put chickpeas in it, provoking a flood.

How are things? Our apartment is gorgeous but full of little flaws that need to be taken care of. My mom is an incredible help, as long as she has company. Poor Brett is not well, both physically and mentally. He has a bad bronchitis and only today is finally seeing a doctor. His cough is really painful. He is also overstretched, doing as usual a wonderful job getting the house ready. But he says he feels "in prison," which is very mortifying for me because I know that things would be different were I more than a wet rag. "Vabbe'." He is also facing the hurdles of the Italian bureaucracy, trying to enroll Zach in school. We visited the school, and from time to time, Zach repeats that he wants to go to school. But first, Brett needs the "permesso di soggiorno" from the police, then the "residenza" and finally a temporary (ha) permit. But nobody told him anything in advance, so each time he goes to an office (once at 6 in the morning, in a line on the sidewalk under the rain in the dark) they send him to another office.

I went three times to the office, and everybody was very nice. I told [...] I have AIDS. He has MS and we traded symptoms. Of the four proposals I gave, one was accepted, two maybe, and one rejected. Not bad. But now I have to write them!

Rome is beautiful and Manu is wonderful. Everybody is anxiously waiting for you and Jimmy. I miss you. A big hug, Gio.

The new apartment, three-quarters furnished, had an old-world grandeur that made me feel I was a privileged guest. I couldn't believe we were going to be living amidst all the curlicued, marble-topped, gilt-framed furnishings. This palazzo enhanced the unreality of the entire transition, and its spacious splendor, so clearly an extravagant but meager compensation for the narrowings imposed on us by Giovanni's illness, would have to be forfeited, I knew, once the illness ran its full course. The two were inextricably linked; one allowed the other. The end of one would mean the end of the other. This apartment, unfortunately, would be part of the temporariness, something to not grow too attached to, a place not to endow with roots.

Soon after we moved in—a simple initial undertaking since our shipment wasn't due in Naples for at least another month—I succeeded in enrolling Zach in the local public preschool that Stefano had attended when he was Zach's age. When Giovanni, Zach, and I visited the school two weeks before, Giovanni had reverted to his former wheelchair shyness, insisting that it be parked far from the view of the classrooms. Once Zach was enrolled, a routine began to emerge. I'd take him to school at 8:30, buy the newspapers, return home to prepare Giovanni's infusion and breakfast, which he'd have simultaneously while reading *La Stampa*. By 11:00, Giovanni would either leave for work for two or three hours or not leave for work. Either way, between 11:00 and 1:00, I'd usually take care of domestic and setting-up-house chores or run errands since everything shut down between 1:30 and 4:30.

One of my almost daily errands was to the doctor to pick up prescriptions and to the pharmacy to have them filled. Although the price of prescriptions was very low (at most $2.50 per prescription), the quantities given were very small—between five and twenty tablets. Giovanni was taking up to fourteen prescriptions, comprising thirty-eight pills, a day, for which at least one of them needed to be refilled each day.

At one o'clock, I'd prepare lunch for Giovanni and me, and for Stefano if it were the time of week when he was staying with us. Afternoons were usually spent with Stefano or, if he wasn't with us, doing something in a reclining position like reading or taking a nap with Giovanni, until I had to pick Zach up from school at 4:30. The hours between five and eight o'clock were the most taxing and dreaded for me. Zach, deprived by school of his afternoon nap and struggling with a new language, was usually zombie-like for the first hour of our return home. I was trapped in his web of imperiousness and inconsolability while I struggled to make dinner, all the while listening to Giovanni watching TV or talking on the phone with friends. Friday nights were somewhat easier since we'd continued our tradition of having Sabbath dinners to which we invited friends or family, who always entertained Zach while I was in the kitchen. I'd long given up on the possibility of Giovanni intervening during one of the at least twenty times that Zach shouted, "Daddy!" and Giovanni's social repose and familial obliviousness during these hours made me want a new life. As in New York and Fire Island, all was quiet by 8:30, and my solitude felt like a punishment rather than a reward.

Giovanni's family and many friends always asked me, "What can I do to help?" to which I always replied, "Help me figure out a way in which you can help. You've seen how it goes here. Any ideas?" Only the question itself resurfaced from time to time, a reminder of the genuine concern, and of the relative insularity of the problem. When I'd gone to the doctor and he told me I had bronchitis, he advised, "You must try to stay in bed and certainly not go outdoors for at least a week." I could only laugh.

Rome, November 14, 1991

Dearest Sam,

Today is a rainy day in Rome but not cold. This morning, I had to go very early to the Vigili Urbani to get my papers for the residency. Then I came back and slept some more. Right now, I'm just back from shopping for food with Brett (Stefano is coming for lunch). Brett is not well at all. His bronchitis is not going away. He has a lot of phlegm. When he coughs, he feels like a stab on his left side. Today he's going to see the doctor again. This illness is preventing him from enjoying Rome much and he's also worried.

Starting tomorrow, I'll have a six-hour infusion every day! (plus the one-hour infusion of DHPG). That means no social life anymore, but I'm glad we're starting this aggressive therapy against diarrhea. A lot of nutrients, replenishing substances, plus a shot twice a day of a strong drug, plus other assorted liquids. Let's hope! Anyhow, tonight there will be the Last Supper of the Buried Alive. We (but maybe not Brett) are going to Giovanna's, who invited us for dinner with Alex S. and his wife. And it was all for Brett! I still hope he can make it. He and Stefano went to Manu's for a special reiki seminar that they enjoyed very much. Stefano was so sarcastic about it during our weekend in Porvietoli that Manu could tell there was interest there! We have settled on a three-day pattern with Stefano plus rotating weekends. I would have preferred a week at a time, and Stefano asked for two weeks in a row! But Giovanna vetoed it, and I can understand it. Anyway, he seems happy and adjusted and enjoying Brett's maternal care.

Between Brett and me it's ups and downs as usual. Tomorrow he's starting individual therapy. Thursday is couple therapy. Whoa! I wasn't looking forward to this but I understand it's necessary. I've got to become more attentive and he looser. The other night he was in a rage because when he came back from his (first) night out, Zach had not even had a bath and wasn't wearing his pajamas. To punish me, he slept on the sofa. I think he exaggerates, but basically, he's right. I wish he could accept me the way I am, though.

I forgot to tell you that I'm on a strict diet. No fruit (except bananas), no vegetables (except carrots and potatoes), no cheese (except gruyere and Parmesan), no milk. That doesn't leave much of the things I like best.

We are establishing a routine, and this house is perfect for that. Stefano is a real slob, but Brett is determined to shape him up. We all miss you a lot, and I more than everybody else. A big big hug. Gio.

After a thorough examination and review of Giovanni's medical records, Giovanni's doctor urged him to start a six-hour infusion of nutrients every day, for which he assumed that Giovanni would want to be admitted to the hospital. We pleaded with him, however, to make some kind of arrangement for a nurse to come to the house to do it, informing him that I could monitor and dismantle it. He consented, and every afternoon at six o'clock, Armando arrived to set up the infusion, which looked like an enormous udder loping on a pole. Giovanni and I had mulled over the various six-hour slots in which he could have the infusion, and decided that early evening would be least inconvenient. If he were to have it in the morning, he wouldn't be able to go to work at all; if he were to have it in the afternoon, it would preclude the possibility of us ever going out for a stroll. (As it turned out, we only went out in the afternoon once more.) Early evening, we agreed, would be best, since Giovanni rarely went out at night and could, in fact, sleep through half of the infusion.

Unfortunately, the assembly of the infusion took about an hour and thus the infusion, for which Armando had to carefully measure out and pour more than twelve liquids into the udder, didn't actually begin its drip until about seven o'clock. When Armando arrived, Zach would get his doctor kit and one of his stuffed animals. Armando would give Zach a mask and a few of the discards, and Zach would imitate the procedure with great zeal. The infusion usually ended up taking eight hours since it was impossible to get the drip rate exact, i.e., calculating and monitoring the flow of about two gallons worth of drips so that they'd finish in precisely six hours, and the rule was better too slow than too fast. I would set the alarm clock for 1:00 in the morning, hoping to disassemble the infusion, only to find that some liquid remained. I would reset the alarm for another half hour and continued with this tortuous process, reminiscent of sleep-deprived nights during Zach's infancy, until 3:00 or 4:00 in the morning. When the infusion was finally finished, I'd still have to go to the kitchen to prepare the heparin solution, which had to be refrigerated, in order to flush out the catheter. Armando also came twice a week at 6:30 in the morning to draw blood. The DHPG and neupogen took Giovanni's white cells on a roller-coaster ride, and the count had to be monitored through blood analysis twice a week at a minimum. Miraculously, both Zach and Giovanni managed to sleep through these predawn visits.

I did manage to go with Giovanni to Giovanna's apartment for dinner with Alex Stille. It was Giovanni's only visit to his son's house, as it was a fifth-floor walk-up; I had to carry him piggyback up the last three flights. It was the most "normal" evening we had had in months. The conversation was expansive, polemic, and never touched upon AIDS. The Stilles offered us a ride home, and as soon as we entered our apartment building, Giovanni hobbled up the twelve stairs, breathless, and collapsed on the bed. I undressed him, tucked him in, and spent some time with Manu, who had babysat with Zach.

Manu had invited Stefano and me to participate in two reiki lessons that she was teaching in the "Yoga Room" in her apartment, a large spare room that had been bared of all furnishings and strewn with mats and pillows and small rugs. It was here that Manu taught both yoga and reiki, and she was encouraging Stefano and me to learn reiki as a kind of spiritual balm for what she saw as our individual sequestered pain, and to inject a new element into my life that had nothing to do with "arrangements." I liked the idea of Stefano exploring a dimension so rarely explored by children his age, as well as the idea of the two of us having a shared project. We attended the two introductory classes, in which there were eight other participants. Each of us took turns lying on our backs, surrounded by the other nine, who began the process of very lightly placing their hands on our bodies in order to allow the mutual exchange of heat and energy to begin. The hour had a slightly cosmic resonance, and Stefano's initial cynicism had completely evanesced by the end of the first session. I thoroughly enjoyed it, for the stillness, the tender, focused physical attention that my body was receiving.

The formal training itself was expensive and required a weekend commitment. I couldn't see how I could break out of my nest for an entire weekend. It could have been possible, perhaps, if Manu had been the one to step in and take care of Zach and Giovanni, but she was the instructor for the training. In addition, Stefano had just abandoned his violin for the saxophone, there was talk of horseback riding lessons, and I was concerned that one more pursuit involving discipline would be overkill. As far as the money, there were several banal acquisitions that seemed more compelling: a color television, a VCR, and couple therapy for Giovanni and me. We decided to put reiki on hold.

Rome, November 22, 1991

Dear Sam,

The other day your second letter arrived like a ray of sunlight on a bad day. I was in pain for a colic that took me like a red-hot pliers in the front and back. I had to be taken to the hospital because the painkillers didn't do much. They feared an ulcer that could become perforated. Mysteriously, the pain went away, and now I'm happy. Tonight, I'm cooking risotto with tartufi. Wouldn't you like to be here?

Tuesday, Brett and I went to couple therapy. Now he has second thoughts. At any rate, we'll try it. The first session was mostly dedicated to our background: families and our relationship. Sometimes I'm tired of talking of myself, like with the medical visits. Today I saw the neurologist and for the tenth time, I repeated my story. Of course, with the couple therapist there's a purpose. But it's tiresome. Brett spoke more than I did. I was cast as the villain. But . . .

November 23. As I was saying about couple therapy, this was only the first session, and it's bound to develop in unforeseen directions. It's probably going to be useful. But I dread the "medicalization" of our life. There's so much of it already that's unavoidable.

We had trouble because the hospital didn't want to pay our valiant nurse twice, now that he's actually doing a double job. Finally, they found a very Italian solution: it will appear as if he comes here twice a day. Hopefully, in a week or so, the seven-hour infusion should be over, and my life a little more normal. At night I wake up so many times to urinate, and thrash about the rest of the time, that Brett was forced to go sleeping in the living room. But being Friday night, the street was very noisy so he couldn't sleep!

I miss New York and I miss you. However, Rome is beautiful and it's such a joy to have Stefano around, even if I end up not seeing much of him. A big hug. Gio.

Giovanni did go off the mega-infusion after three weeks. He wasn't any worse, but he wasn't any better. His doctor wanted him admitted to the hospital. He felt that numerous analyses and examinations needed to be taken throughout the day, that two blood tests a week were not enough, and it was simply impossible to do more from the house. Besides, he was lucky enough to have gotten Giovanni a bed. We consented. We had to cancel our second appointment with the couple therapist, which may have been for the best. His approach was that of a full excavation, bringing in each family member, one at a time, to obtain the most comprehensive and multiperspective history possible. In other circumstances, perhaps I would have been more amenable to such an approach. But with the clock ticking, I was looking for more superficial, pragmatic solutions. While I was packing his bag for the hospital, Giovanni advised me, "Don't forget to pack towels, pajamas, soap, and toilet paper. They don't provide them here. This is Italy."

Spallanzani Hospital for Infectious Diseases is a cluster of buildings housed within a complex of other specialized medical facilities. It must have been beautiful once, lush, resort-like. Roman pines and palms tower over the uniformly golden brick and terra-cotta-roofed buildings, which are amply separated by lawns. However, only the pines have managed to escape the hideous neglect that has severely desiccated this walled-in city of the ill.

Giovanni shared his room with nine other AIDS patients, seven of whom were clearly heroin addicts. The room had no telephones, televisions, partitions; just ten beds, ten metal storage lockers, and a few stray plastic chairs for visitors. There was no waiting room, and the corridor leading to the locked ward had no seats. Visiting hours were from 3:00 to 4:00 each day. Only one visitor was permitted at a time. A special permit could be obtained in order to extend the visiting hours. This "How To Punish the Ill for Being Ill" ambience took some getting used to, and Giovanni's ten-day stay wasn't sufficient time for me. To say that Spallanzani resembled a prison is too obvious. Besides, I've never been in a prison.

Giovanni was calm, relaxed, concentrated on writing the article for *L'Espresso* about his life with AIDS, the only article he wrote for the magazine while in Rome. When the editor had proposed that he write the piece, Giovanni said he would have to think about it. For several weeks we talked about it, the implications it could have for Stefano and Zach, what it would mean for Giovanni to go public, to commit his illness to paper. He was ambivalent. All of us were ambivalent. But for once I struggled for reticence in the belief that this decision was Giovanni's alone. When he was admitted to the hospital, he considered the possibility that his strategy of "keeping the illness small" was no longer effective. Now was the time. He wrote the article in its entirety during his stay in Spallanzani. He also lost it. When we arrived home from the hospital, and I unpacked, it was nowhere to be found. We drove back to the hospital, checked the locker, the garbage bins, the nurses' station. It was gone. Giovanni thought that he had thrown it away unconsciously once he was leaving the hospital, feeling a resurgence of hope and with it the redeployment of old strategies. He hadn't been ready after all.

Rome, December 5, 1991

Dear Sam,

I'm writing you from the hospital where I was sent yesterday to have me "under control." But I can't quite understand what control they're talking about. They don't even know that I need to be fed via I/V! Come the doctors, pompous and solemn, read my chart, point out to each other something obvious, then leave.

I have to tell you that I feel quite discouraged.

It's like being back at square one, in September. I lost weight, diarrhea became explosive and much more frequent. It seems one can't get out of this situation. More and more my hopes rest on Switzerland. I was going to visit my grandmother today and tomorrow take Stefano to a Marcel Marceau show on Sunday, and go to Manu's concert on the 16th. My editor asked me to write about me, and I'm torn. I haven't consulted Giovanna yet. Brett won't talk. I have already started writing anyway because it's good for me. But I'm so hard, I almost can't feel! I also try ill-advised jokes, like talking about how expensive Fire Island was because it was supposed to be the Last Summer: "Next year we go to Atlantic City!"

And you and Jimmy Jimmizino? You don't talk about it at all! Please do come. It would be a ray of light in the Roman Winter of Mr. Forti. Love G.

13

Christmas was approaching. Giovanni's new-fledged observance of Judaism was a break from the traditions of his family, all of whom celebrated Christmas in its commercial manifestations, even though his mother, father, and younger sister are practicing Buddhists. I'd never before celebrated Christmas, with its effusions of gift-giving and aftermath of crumpled wrapping paper. I was looking forward to the promise of family gatherings and gaiety, particularly since Zach and I had had to light the menorah and exchange gifts without Giovanni, who had been in the hospital for seven of the eight days of Chanukkah.

We bought Stefano a calotes for Christmas, which we kept in a glass cage in the living room. He had wanted a chameleon, but after calling dozens of pet shops in Rome, I came to the conclusion that they either don't exist in Italy or hide exceptionally well. I was told that a calotes is similar to a chameleon, minus the color transmogrifications. I had a hunch, besides, that what interested Stefano most was the reptilian nature of the beast, its potential to either terrify or repulse his friends.

Stefano was spending the Christmas vacation near the town of Amelia, at Cenci, the home of the father of his best friend. After some coaxing, Giovanni relented and we spent Christmas at Cenci too. Giovanni was reluctant to go because of the cold weather and the large gathering of people that Cenci traditionally drew during the Christmas holiday. Giovanni didn't want to have to have his infusion in the midst of a throng.

Cenci is a sprawling, refurbished farmhouse set up like a camp, for which it is used for two weeks in summer—the bedrooms each have at least five beds in them, and one must walk through one bedroom to get to another. Franco, the owner of the house, arranged for us to have the bedroom at the end of the house, separated from the other rooms by what used to be a stable and that was in the process of being converted into a kind of gymnasium. This particular bedroom resembled a studio apartment, complete with a separate bathroom, space heaters, an electric burner for coffee or tea, and a large loft. Given these amenities, Giovanni agreed to go.

The holiday weekend perfectly replicated the weekend spent in Porvietoli: Giovanni huddled around the fireplace, joyful, animated, grateful, always cold, always tired, always struggling. And again, driving back I had to promise him that we wouldn't return until the warm weather arrived.

Our second and final walk in Rome took place on La Befana. Giovanni wanted to take Zach and me to Piazza Navona where each year a festival is held that is reminiscent of the festivals of the saints held in Manhattan's Little Italy and Greenwich Village: stalls redolent with oil frying or festooned with larger-than-life stuffed animals, the sky obstructed by thousands of balloons, the ground straining to sustain the crush of visitors. I was concerned about the distance to be traveled with the wheelchair—Piazza Navona is about five times as far as the Isola Tiberina—and the impact it would have on my hands, but I was so overjoyed that Giovanni was genuinely wanting to go that I decided it would be worth however many blisters and aches I would receive as a result. As we headed for the Piazza, it was clear that most of the pedestrians had the same destination in mind. The crowd grew thicker and thicker, and by the time we reached the narrow street that enters into the Piazza, the human congestion was at a standstill. Giovanni was unabashedly miserable by this time. Over the months, he had been increasingly unable to cope with groups of more than three or four people, and this dense mass was simply too much for him. "I can't continue," he said.

As soon as we entered the Piazza, I parked his wheelchair by the side of the fountain and strode off with Zach on my shoulders. After about a half hour, Zach and I, and one very large Mickey Mouse balloon, wended our way back toward the fountain. From a distance of about fifty feet, my eyes found Giovanni. Amidst the din and tumult that could be heard for blocks around, he was slumped over in his wheelchair fast asleep. I studied him for a few minutes from that distance, trying to objectify him. All that was visible of him was his face, pale and gaunt, drained of color, of life. His once-bushy eyebrows and dark mustache were now sparse, lighter in color, bereft of any sheen. I noticed eye sockets before I noticed his closed eyes. The contours of his torso were concealed by his ultrathick down coat and wool scarf (it was about 55 degrees that day), but the posture was severely concave, as if in an effort to fold in upon itself. From under this cloth bulk, two disproportionately thin legs were clenched together, tight, contracted. I stared at him until he seemed a stranger to me. And as a stranger, he no longer appeared sick, only old. Very, very old.

A friend of Manu's was going on holiday after Christmas and was looking for someone to take care of her puppy. Since Zach was going to be out of school for two weeks, I offered to take the puppy, thinking that it would be a good playmate for Zach. Our cat, Moats, didn't take too kindly to the cowering addition, but she generously kept her distance. I had told Zach and reminded him over the course of the two weeks that the puppy was a temporary guest, that he would have to go back to his home at the end of the holiday.

Three nights before the puppy was to go back home, the calotes died. Two nights before the puppy was to go back home, Moats died. She had been lying under the china cabinet all day, and when I put a plate of cantaloupe under the cabinet next to her and she didn't stir, I knew something was wrong. I pulled her out from under the cabinet and stood her up. In a matter of two days, she had wasted away. She teetered and fell over on her side. After I put Zach to bed, I stayed up with Moats until 1:00 in the morning, stroking her. I knew she wouldn't make it through the night. I prepared a box to put her in later and went to bed, setting the alarm for 4:00 in the morning. When the alarm went off, I went back out into the dining room. She had died. I placed her in the box and put the box on the terrace where Zach wouldn't see her. The following morning, Manu and I took the box to the kennel.

I had a lot of explaining to do to poor Zach. I started with the calotes. When Moats's turn came, I was able to refine the explanation. Dress rehearsals.

Sam and Jimmy arrived toward the end of January, about a week after Giovanni was finally able to visit his grandmother in Florence. He had pressed for both of these visits with uncharacteristic tenacity. They formed part of his unspoken wish list of "Things I Must Do Before I Die": get married, return to Rome, reestablish close ties with his parents and siblings, spend time with his grandmother, have Sam on his native soil once again, visit Israel. At Giovanni's insistence, Sam and Jimmy were to stay with us. Our shipment had arrived just a few days before their arrival, and after forty-eight hours of almost nonstop unpacking, for which Giovanni's contribution this time was one-half a box of books after which he had to lie down, our house felt like a home. After Sam and Jimmy had been with us for two days, Giovanni told me that he needed to have the house restored to its barest human essentials: my caregiving presence and the youthful background clamor of Zach and Stefano. For Giovanni to want Sam to leave the house was, for me, his most potent admission that he was succumbing.

Sam and Jimmy made their rounds of Rome and usually spent an hour or two in the afternoon at the house visiting Giovanni. On one such occasion, Giovanni read aloud to Sam, Jimmy, Stefano, and me the rewritten article for *L'Espresso*, which I had hastily translated into English.

My Life with AIDS

"In the summer of 1991, I rented a house on the ocean on Fire Island, not far from New York. The island is on a long and narrow stretch of sand where cars are not permitted. We had found a rather eccentric house, made entirely of wood, with stairwells, corridors, niches, oddly shaped rooms filled with knickknacks. There was also a deck where we could put a plastic swimming pool for the kids. Besides me and my companion Brett, there were Stefano, age 12, and Zachary, 3. The cost was prohibitive (twice my monthly salary), but it was worth it. We were thinking, after all, that this could be my last summer. My diarrhea was increasing, my weight decreasing, down to 93 pounds. However, I was always able to rejoice at our little family and from the friends who came to visit. I went to the beach for an hour or two, under the beach umbrella, wrapped in towels. I watched Stefano play, like a young hart, with Brett and with my friend Sam. It was a wonderful summer.

"I was diagnosed HIV positive in April 1987, although I think I was infected in the summer of 1981 during a frenetic week in the San Francisco baths. After the diagnosis, I did absolutely nothing.

But when my T4 cells began to drop, the doctors suggested that I start a treatment based on AZT, a toxic drug that at the time was the only one known to slow the replication of the virus. From that moment, my life was announced, every four hours, by a persistent sound: the beep of my pill box, which, over the years, would be filled with various pills, sometimes 10 different types. At first, I took flying leaps to prevent it from beeping in public. Then I relaxed. In New York, to have the 'beeper' was equivalent to admitting you had AIDS. The syndrome was everywhere. It wasn't difficult to become obsessed.

"I opened the *New York Times* to the obituaries (something that seemed rather comic when my grandmother was doing it with her local daily paper) and always came across a couple of AIDS-related deaths. Even those who seem immortal, who last four years, six years, who fight the opportunistic infections like lions with every kind of treatment or simply with transcendental meditation and homeopathy, die in the end. There is a feeling of inevitability.

"The organizations for assistance to those with AIDS were growing by leaps, with budgets in the millions. There were frequent benefits and other initiatives to raise funds. I went to one of them with my boyfriend at that time, James Revson, a worldly scion-journalist of a Jewish aristocratic family. Nudged by him, I bought my first tuxedo and came into contact with a segment of New York society that would be of value to me as a journalist. James had Karposi Sarcoma (KS), a skin cancer that manifests itself with purple lesions. He was always tired, had to take naps, and took taxis to cover distances of even ten blocks. This annoyed me, and I treated him badly.

"The nemesis would arrive at my door only too soon. I tried to avoid writing articles about homosexuality and about AIDS, the two topics always becoming more linked in the collective imagination, but sometimes I couldn't avoid it. One such piece was a large feature on American writers and AIDS. Almost all of those I interviewed at the time are now dead. One of them, Alain Emmanuel Dreuilhe, was living in a loft that he kept almost completely dark, and when I met him, he was lying in bed with an IV dripping through a catheter that had been surgically implanted in his body. I found it horrifying.

"In spite of everything, this funereal atmosphere didn't possess me, at least not consciously. I had fun, traveled, took care of my son, worked. Work enabled me to encounter things and people that otherwise would have been beyond my reach. Slowly, the virus was making its way through my body, and the evidence was in my T4 cell count, always going down. I had to spend one night in the hospital for an excruciating spinal tap. That night, a large priest entered my room and stopped to exchange a few words. When he went away, he left his business card: John Cardinal O'Connor. I thought I had been dreaming, but the nurse confirmed that the arch-reactionary came frequently to visit the AIDS ward.

"The doctors decided to add new medications. I switched from Saint Clare's Hospital and from a brusque and ambitious Brooklyn doctor to St. Luke's Roosevelt with a plump, blond, and prudent doctor. Perhaps too prudent. I now had to pay for the visits, but part of the expenses was reimbursed by my insurance. I had chosen not to tell anyone about my condition except Sam and my sister. But in the summer of

1987, my mother read my diary and slowly the news spread. Besides, it would soon be impossible to hide it.

"In June 1990, I met Brett and his adopted son, Zach. They were living in Brooklyn in a house in a Caribbean neighborhood bordering a huge park, but almost immediately they moved in with me in Greenwich Village. I spent that August in Vermont in a house in the woods with Stefano, Sam, my sister, and a friend of hers. I think back with sadness to those strolls and bicycle rides. Today, I'm no longer able to do such things, and for long walks, I must go in a wheelchair. It was one of the happiest periods of my life. I got to know Brett and his son, between whom there was a bond whose intensity was hard to enter into. Stefano returned to Italy, and I missed him a lot, but his absence was in some measure compensated. Brett took great care of me and I felt the family warmth that I'd almost forgotten. In November, almost immediately after a one-week visit to Italy, we went to California for Thanksgiving. There I had my first breakdown, which I had attributed to the double jet lag. I almost always slept, and the diarrhea started. The friends with whom we were staying, and who didn't know that I was HIV positive, were very upset.

"In June 1991, Brett and I were married in a small synagogue, and through a series of circumstances, the private event ended up being announced on television. Our parents attended, mine coming from Italy and Brett's from Philadelphia, as well as our friends. The ceremony was a traditional one with a huppah held up by our dearest friends and the glass broken underfoot. But during the reception, which took place in our apartment, I had to go into the bedroom to take a nap. Again, at night, for our mini-honeymoon (friends had paid for a night in the elegant Hotel Carlyle). As soon as we arrived, at 7:00, I had to sleep again for two hours.

"I was saddened by our having to put a stop to our adoption plans. We had gone through the necessary paperwork to adopt another baby, and I was so filled with joy that it would have been the child of both of us and thought how much this mutual adoption would create an even stronger bond between Brett and me. It would have been wonderful for Zach to have a little sister. But with my deteriorating health, Brett convinced me that it wasn't going to be. There were other reasons for sadness. I found out in the newspapers that James Revson had died. It was a shock because our mutual friends had told me nothing about his condition, also because he had asked that I not see him in the hospital nor attend his funeral. Such rancor pained me, but perhaps there was good reason. More or less at the same time, Brett's former companion died.

"Things were not going well. Already in November, I was not at all well. The diarrhea started, accompanied by fever. In August, on Fire Island, the fevers became very high and the diarrhea explosive. I often soiled the entire toilet bowl and also the floor. Sometimes I did it in my underwear. I was growing weaker and thinner before my very eyes. By the end of the month, I almost looked like a concentration camp survivor. And then my tortuous nights began, waking up constantly to pee. I am aware that these are not very attractive details, but they were a part of my life in those months. I began to get tired more often and wasn't able to stay on the beach for long periods of time nor to contribute to family chores. For Brett, unfortunately, the vacation on Fire Island was exhausting, all the more so because two days a week he commuted to New York to work.

"I never allowed morbid thoughts to take over but I knew what was happening. I decided to talk to Stefano, who had flown in from Italy to spend the month with us, but as it turned out, there was a block in the conversation because I never pronounced the word AIDS, and he didn't at all understand that my conversation about the infection pertained to this. In the end, it was necessary for Brett to speak to him clearly in order for him to understand the scope of what was happening.

"Very alarmed in the beginning of September, Brett insisted that I go into the hospital. At first, I was terrified, but then almost relieved at the idea that someone would be taking care of me 24 hours a day. My roommate, separated from me only by a plastic curtain, was a Hispanic drug addict named Manuel. He was a difficult roommate. He ranted a lot. At night he would call to the nurse, 'I want a blanket!' He did this seven times one night until the stock of spare blankets had been depleted. He called out for stronger painkillers. 'But give them time to take effect,' the poor nurse protested. 'You took them only 40 minutes ago.' He kept the TV on at a high volume and constantly switched channels. He often dozed, always with the TV on. Even when his entire noisy family came to visit, the screen continued its babble.

"Almost immediately, with a minor operation, I had a catheter inserted in my stomach, with a plastic tube that went up to my neck. A simple device but one that changed the way I viewed my body. I felt like the bionic man. This protuberance assured that I could no longer hide my condition, almost like a black whose blackness is evident and not like a gay who can hide his gayness if he wants. Brett came every day. I think that for him this was, on the whole, a period of repose.

"In the beginning, I didn't want to see anyone, then I had visitors. I was, as always, in good spirits, but I tired very easily. I asked to be transferred to another room, but Manuel beat me to it and decided to have himself released from the hospital against the advice of the doctors. I hoped that my new roommate would be someone with whom I could have conversations; instead, an elderly black man arrived with missing teeth, very quiet. I was uneasy about the racism I was discovering in me, but it was difficult to fight off.

"I was always hooked up to an I/V, twenty-four hours a day, a kind of nutrient breast from which I could never detach myself. When I was released from the hospital, a nurse came to our house and soon turned Brett into a master paramedic. Every three days, my needle was changed to prevent infection and a new one was put in.

"In this situation, many people thought it was absurd for me and Brett to persist in the idea of moving to Rome. I was using 40 pills and various accessories (needles, tubings, vials of sodium chloride, etc.), rather complicated to transport (we were afraid about customs). But there were several reasons not to abandon the idea, the principal of which was that it had already been a year that I'd been separated from Stefano, and I wanted to be with him again. In addition, I wasn't in the best condition to work, and it would have been worse as a correspondent than as an editor without a by-line. The moving company packed everything for us and, therefore, there wasn't too much difficulty. Brett, as always, displayed prodigious energy. A dear friend gave a farewell party (a farewell to more than five years of life). Naturally, there were the usual surprises: good friends who couldn't make it and strangers who were the life of the party. Then we left.

"To tell the truth, my desire to return to Italy was not great, and, above all, I really wanted to remain in New York, but, in general, I never look back. In Rome, an apartment in Trastevere found by my mother was waiting for us, almost ready, traditionally furnished, and with a terrace. It seemed paradoxical that while psychologically my focus was narrowing more and more, and physically I had to drastically reduce my activities, I found myself now living in the largest home I'd ever had. It's wonderful to have my mother and sister living nearby. One nap a day became two: one in the morning, either during or after the IV, and one in the afternoon immediately following lunch. I go to bed at 8:30 at night, hours that are not conducive to an intense social and cultural life.

"Everything grew worse when the doctors in Italy gave me an IV of nutrients that lasted seven hours a day, along with a very rigid diet: no dairy products, vegetables, or fruits with a very few exceptions. Besides, my condition started to deteriorate again as in September. Dr. Sette, my doctor at Spallanzani, decided to have me admitted to the hospital. I was put in a huge room in which almost all the other patients were drug addicts, but quiet at least, and the nurses were kind and efficient. The doctors proved to be good but arrogant. Every morning, they arrived at my bedside and read my chart. I didn't understand: couldn't they have done this in their office? 'This young man is not able to eat,' proclaimed one of them. 'I eat incredibly well.' 'Oh really?' he replied, surprised. I wondered how he had arrived at this notion. Nevertheless, the fact remains that something was being done right because my condition was improving gradually, at least in terms of my weight and frequency of diarrhea.

"Being in the hospital forced me to confront death. Not liking to talk about AIDS in general, for me death has always been the ultimate taboo. But now it is inevitable. I have made a will, for example. I even wrote that I didn't want any extraordinary life-sustaining measures taken. But this is something that I still can't quite believe. I won't be any more? Certainly, as human beings we are all always headed toward death, but I am a few steps closer. The only way to avoid tormenting oneself is to reconcile oneself with it, mentally asking forgiveness, as well as forgiving, and to hope that something remains.

"I am writing the bulk of these lines in the hospital. Just outside my window are two Roman pines. I watch them at sunrise and sunset and my heart fills with joy. I am, as always, optimistic."

During the reading, I continually watched Stefano's face for signs of emotional activity, but Stefano had inherited his father's gift for stolidness. It was anyone's guess as to what, if anything, was churning inside.

Sam and Jimmy were going to be in Rome for Giovanni's birthday. Nevertheless, when I asked Giovanni what he wanted to do for his birthday, he told me, "I want to go out to dinner with you, to a quiet restaurant with linen tablecloths and candles." The challenge was to find a local restaurant that opened at 7:30, in order to be home close to Giovanni's bedtime. I made some phone inquiries and located a restaurant whose maître d' promised to let us in at 7:30. When we arrived, the person on the floor wouldn't admit us, claiming he had no idea what we were talking about; we spent the next half hour bumping through Trastevere in the wheelchair, trying to find a restaurant that would stray from its tradition of opening at 8:30. I was tempted to give up and go home but couldn't since Sam and I had planned a surprise party for Giovanni. We had invited everyone in Rome whom Giovanni knew with the stipulation that they arrive punctually at 8:30 and leave no later than 9:30.

Giovanni and I finally found a restaurant and had a wonderfully romantic dinner; I refused to be concerned about the dire fatigue that was inscribed on his face. When we arrived home and entered the dining room, everyone jumped out of the kitchen, and Stefano lit the fireworks on the terrace, illuminating a giant "Happy Birthday Giovanni" that had been sprayed onto the terrace wall. Giovanni was instantly sentimental. He knew that another "last" had just taken place.

Sam and Jimmy left on the 10th, missing Manu's birthday party by two days. In order to enable Giovanni to attend her party, Manu had arranged to have it at 7:30 in a Chinese restaurant down the street. When Giovanni, Zach, and I arrived, there were about twenty other guests. I knew that it could be at least an hour before everyone settled down to think about ordering dinner. I called the waitress over and ordered dinner for the three of us. By 8:00, Giovanni showed his usual signs of needing to be in bed instantly. His face looked like a study in the annihilation of color, and it seemed that somebody had just clicked off a light. We left before the others had ordered. It was Giovanni's last social outing.

February 1992

For Brett

People come to visit me. I'm like an idol; I wait. I don't require much: some conversation, some food, some medicines. I don't move. Like any proper idol,

I stay. I fear the day that a novel Abraham will come and smash the idols. So, I try not to attract the attention. I don't make miracles. No lightning in the sky. I don't require sacrifices; I don't require gifts (but I'm very happy when I get them). All in all, I'm a very inconspicuous idol.

You are also an idol but, on the contrary, a tempestuous one. Your fury is terrible and explodes more and more often. Materially, you don't require much either. You are a very rapid idol and when you go through a room everything is neat and when you go through a kitchen there are meals made with many courses. You make miracles. On the other hand, you do require something: attention. When you don't get the attention you need you become very angry. I then try to shrink, to make myself invisible, not understanding that maybe this will make you even more mad. Sometimes you resort to the threat of leaving me and I feel crushed, nonexistent. Maybe, after all, you are already the idol smasher.

14

One morning in the beginning of February, I was cleaning out my backpack—my portable attic—and found Giovanni's original response to my personal ad with its opening line: "Sure, I can change a diaper!" I had an idea, although it was radically different from what Giovanni had had in mind when he wrote this line. I went to the bedroom where Giovanni was awake but not feeling up to getting out of bed, and said, "How would you feel about wearing a diaper?" He looked at me as if I were crazy. I continued, "Your diarrhea always arrives unannounced, and you walk around with a fixed minimum of anxiety wondering when the diarrhea will come and whether you'll make it to a bathroom in time. And let's face it, often you don't." He agreed to wear a disposable diaper at night and during the day if he were going out of the house. He'd already been wearing inner liners, shaped like shoe pads, in his underwear for about a month to absorb the occasional trickle of amber-colored urine that escaped him unawares several times a day. One of the very few things capable of making Giovanni angry was defecating in his pants. He found it humiliating, it stripped him of his dignity, and he hated to have to ask me to clean him since he didn't have the physical equilibrium.

The article in *L'Espresso* appeared on February 16, the day after Giovanni came down with acute laryngitis. It was the cover story, and moreover, Giovanni's face was plastered all over Rome, along with the headline, "Diary of an AIDS

Patient," on the enlarged magazine cover photos that hang from the city's newspaper kiosks and streetlight poles. The telephone rang perpetually, the mailbox was flooded with letters, telegrams, and small parcels.

A few days after the article appeared, Giovanni was asked to be interviewed on television. The interview was haunting: wraith-like, with a rasping, breathless voice that was barely audible and at least one octave higher than usual, and an expression of pain and remorse that had finally reached the outward destination of his face, Giovanni spoke, not with strength but with a kind of humble resignation, always clear and straightforward but at times incredulous that the person whom he was talking about, who was dying and leaving behind two young children, a companion, and a world whose marvels had been largely untouched, was not someone other than himself. Giovanni was now on the other side.

Almost immediately after the interview, Giovanni's health went into a rapid decline. The slight cough that accompanied his laryngitis became more persistent and mucus-filled; his fevers and bouts of diarrhea were at an all-time high, and his energy level at an all-time low. Then, the brividi—tremors—started. Two or three times a day, Giovanni's temperature would leap from subnormal (96) to 104 in a period of an hour or an hour and a half, during which time his entire body went into severe tremors. I would jump on the bed, cradle his head in my crossed legs, and try to massage the rigidity out of his body while he grabbed at me, squeezed me, bit me, in an effort to expel the formidable pain. He cried, screamed, "Non ne posso più" (I can't take any more), and by the end of the ordeal, the sheets were soaked in sweat, urine, and feces. These bouts undid Giovanni, left him lifeless. He no longer tried to get to the bathroom and had to be carried to the living room sofa for a change of atmosphere. He could no longer make himself heard. I kept a bell by his side so that if he needed anything, he could signal. The bell went off every fifteen minutes, for a diaper change or a glass of water.

The episodes completely undid me as well. Their duration, and the aftermath of changing sheets and diapers and cleaning Giovanni, comprised almost three hours. If one took place in the morning, by the time it subsided, it was close to noon and Giovanni hadn't even had his infusion or morning medications. I would become so flustered that I couldn't even remember what medications I had to give him. At this point, I had to make a chart.

	WAKE UP	LUNCH	4:00	DINNER	BED
Diflucan	X (every other day)				
Lederfolin	X			X	
Myambutol	X	X		X	
Bactrim	X				
Humatin	2X	2X		2X	2X
Ferrograd	X			X	
Cladersol	X	X		X	X
Ciproxin	X		X	X	
Lyseen	X			X	
Rifadin				2X	
Tachipirina	X		X		X
Dalmadorm				X	
Imodium	X	X		X	
Cortigen B	X				

I finally gave up trying to manage this situation on my own. Giovanni could not be left alone for a minute, and I could not be left alone with Giovanni when Zach was in the house in the event that Giovanni had an attack. I called Silvia and Manu, and we organized a schedule. Silvia would come every morning from 11:00 until 1:00 to enable me to do the grocery shopping and errands, or else, she would run the errands, and I would remain with Giovanni. Manu would come every afternoon at 5:00, when I returned from school with Zach, and stay until I put Zach to bed.

At the end of the second day of Giovanni's brividi, I called our new visiting doctor, Ciccio, whom we had obtained through a social services agency when the hospital could no longer provide us with Armando; he had given us his beeper number in case of an emergency. "Call me the next time Giovanni has brividi," he told me. "I'll be over immediately to draw blood." Ciccio was younger than us but venerable with competence and witnessed pain. He often dropped by to see how Giovanni was doing, and his devotion and attentiveness gave me the impression that he had something almost personal at stake in Giovanni's health.

On the third day of the brividi, Ciccio arrived in the middle of an attack to draw blood for analysis. He returned a few hours later with the news that Giovanni had septicemia, a type of blood poisoning, and would have to go into the hospital immediately. I packed his bag, not bothering to change him out of his nightgown before the taxi arrived.

February 23, 1992

Dearest Sam,
    Your visit was a treat for me. How much I miss you! I'm in the hospital but there is some hope. Love love love Gio.

In addition, the I/Vs of DHPG and nutrients, Giovanni was now receiving three I/Vs a day of Tenacid, an antibiotic, to counter the septicemia. With the exception of one remark, "I want to go to Switzerland," which he repeated in a rasping falsetto whisper over and over again, Giovanni had little else to say. He lay in bed with an attitude of child-like obstinacy. On his second day in the hospital, I called the doctor directly in Switzerland. He spoke no English or French, and I spoke no German. I had to hang up the phone and make a series of calls to friends to try and track down a German in Rome. Once found, I asked him to be my interlocutor as I outlined to the doctor the history and present status of Giovanni's health in order to see if we could come directly to him in Switzerland, and as soon as possible. Although the doctor clearly recognized the urgency of the situation, at the same time, he said that he couldn't accept Giovanni in his present condition and that it would be advisable to wait at least until the septicemia was under control and the diarrhea had abated somewhat. I related the doctor's advice to Giovanni and reminded him that he was indeed improving each day. By the second day in the hospital, he'd had brividi only once, and by the third day, they were gone.

Giovanni did not respond to my explanation. I assumed that he'd accepted it. When I arrived on the morning of the fifth day, Giovanni asked me to get him a pair of socks. "Why, are your feet cold?" "No," he replied. "I'm getting dressed. I checked myself out I refused all medication this morning." I started to cry. "Why are you doing this?" I screamed at him. "Why can't you wait just a little bit longer?" "I want to go to Switzerland." I realized that the hope contained in this sentence was unshakeable, and I packed his bag.

When we arrived home, I put Giovanni in bed and said to him, "I'm calling the doctor in Switzerland. If he refuses to see you, do you promise to go back to the hospital?" "Let's see what the doctor says."

The doctor agreed to see Giovanni on Monday. He told me to bring the antibiotics and to use them only if the brividi started up again. "I can't promise anything," was his final remark. I ordered plane tickets for Saturday and hotel reservations for Giovanni, Zach, Manu, and me. I also called Ciccio to ask him if he could get ahold of Tenacid as well as infusions of nutrients for us to take with us to Switzerland. He said he'd do his best. Several hours later, he arrived with twenty-five boxes of Tenacid and ten bottles of Soycal, potassium, and glucose. Five suitcases wouldn't have been sufficient to hold the supplies, and the large bottles of nutrients were glass. Ciccio recommended that we not transport the nutrients. "Four days without them is not going to make a tremendous difference," he said. I picked up Zach from school and notified his teacher that he would not be in class the following Monday, Tuesday, or Wednesday because we were going to Switzerland. She said, "What a wonderful place for a vacation!" Stefano came to the house that afternoon to see his father off. It would be the last time Giovanni and his son would see each other.

We had two contiguous rooms at the Panorama Hotel in Feusisberg, about fifteen minutes away from the clinic in Freienbach. One room was for Zach and Manu, the other for Giovanni and me. Zach and Giovanni had to be supervised twenty-four hours a day. Manu and I rotated during the day. One would take Zach outside where there was a playground, a forest, and a petting zoo on the hotel grounds, or to the jacuzzi in the hotel's gymnasium. The other would stay in the room with Giovanni, massaging him, giving him water, reading aloud to him, changing his diaper, and trying to make sense out of the partial thoughts that his lips were able to push out of his mouth, suspended like a feather in a vacuum, awaiting the breath of now-inaccessible language to give them weight, movement, direction.

Manu and I took two-hour shifts. With nothing to do or think about outside of Zach's and Giovanni's fields of need, an intensity of concentration and almost effortless efficiency emerged. The world became two hotel rooms and a small patch of outdoors. All material needs—food, linens, periodicals—could be had by picking up the phone. And Giovanni's quiet, shallow breathing set the pulse of this world. Even Zach abided by the hushed rhythm when he entered the rooms, as if he had intuited that here he was not the center, nor the controlling force. Something tangibly transcendent had infused this island, and Zach deferred to it without any parental explanation. This visceral harmony, this immense stillness that permeated all enterprise was death's whisper, gentle, unmenacing, a taste of the sweeter portion of her fruit.

By Sunday evening, Giovanni's brividi had started up again, and I began the infusions of Tenacid. By Monday morning, he had gone through all the diapers we'd brought with us. Manu and Zach went into the town proper while I took Giovanni by taxi to his first treatment at the clinic. The treatment was exactly as had been described. Giovanni lay on a table while a pint of blood was drawn and mixed with ozone. The blood was then reinjected, which Giovanni said burned throughout his body. Then he was given an intramuscular injection of Carciviren, as well as two oral doses of Rovital-V, one a gel that had to be smeared against his gums, the other drops that he had to swallow, which he complained tasted like bird piss. In addition, the doctor gave us a homeopathic medicine for Giovanni's diarrhea. Throughout the treatment, the doctor would look at me and shake his head, making a "Tsk, tsk" sound with his tongue. I wasn't expecting the treatment to be able to do anything at this late stage either.

Giovanni, on the other hand, had consolidated all of his remaining faith and strength into the treatment. When we arrived back at the hotel, he insisted on having lunch at the restaurant and heartily ate a plate of white rice and cooked carrots, never taking off his down coat. When, by evening, he had felt no improvement, Giovanni retreated entirely into the coils of his illness, letting it have its way with a complete absence of resistance, defiance, or delusion. Gone were his occasional smile, his desire to be fed or read to, his attempts to get to the bathroom. Often, he didn't even bother to tell us that his diaper was soiled. All of his systems seemed to have atrophied. The few times he spoke, he hung impaled in the middle of a sentence, at a loss for the words that would render it complete but still incomprehensible.

Manu and I both knew that it was a matter of days or weeks. After Zach and Giovanni were asleep, we would spend the rest of the evening sitting with a bottle of wine in the carpeted corridor outside of the two rooms (we always had to be within earshot of both of them) and try to understand what we could do to help Giovanni. The meaning of "help" had been entirely transformed. It no longer had to do with nourishing or fortifying his physical and emotional survival mechanisms; rather, it had to do with helping to tuck him gently into the silence. We sat with Giovanni, reminding him of our proximity through massages or a finger interlocked around one of his. He seemed to want little more, and we didn't know what else we could do.

On the last afternoon in Switzerland, we decided to try to take Giovanni for a stroll in the wheelchair. Something—a desire to give Giovanni some fresh air, a bout of nostalgia for a family outing, a lapse in our acceptance of his imminent death—led us to this mistake. Giovanni was limp as we tried to dress him, although he immediately stiffened as soon as Manu opened the lobby door, and he felt the chilled air. He never once looked out at the mountains, the lake, the sky. After fifteen minutes, he managed to say in an imperious whisper, "I want to go back to the room." When we reached the parking lot of the hotel, three octogenarians were being helped out of a car filled with canes and wheelchairs. The movements of these more justifiable owners of such accessories were identical to those of Giovanni, who was less than half their age.

Manu and I both prayed that Giovanni would not decide just then to break his inward gaze and see these brutal reflections of himself. It was a cruel moment. Rather, the cruelty of the past year had been distilled into that moment. But perhaps Giovanni had already known this and didn't need to see it, or anything else, anymore.

When we returned to Rome the following evening, Giovanni was carried immediately to bed at 7:30. He had been made almost insensible by the constant shiftings that were necessary to get us from a hotel in Feusisberg to our bedroom in Rome. Zach followed an hour later, and Manu left at 9:30. There was peace in the house; I sat at my desk and listened to the answering machine, opened mail, made my lists, caught up. At 10:30, it occurred to me that Giovanni hadn't made a noise or rung the bell since he had been put in bed. I went to the bedroom to check on him. He was sleeping peacefully, though his diaper was soiled. I started to change him. He didn't stir. I raised his arm and let it go; it dropped. I whispered in his ear to squeeze my hand if he could hear me. No response. I climbed onto the bed and clutched his face, whispering and singing softly in his ear. He is dying, I thought. I spent an hour in this way, peaceful, calm, ready, troubled only by the thought that perhaps I was being selfish in hoarding his last moments, that Manu deserved to take part in this final easeful passage after what we'd shared in Switzerland. I called her and said, "Giovanni is dying," and she replied, quietly, "I'm coming." She joined me on the bed, and we spent the next two hours stroking Giovanni and talking to him soothingly. I remember thinking how this night, this setting, this calm, would be a perfect death. Then Giovanni coughed. That cough revivified him; his eyes fluttered open, he brought his arm up to his chest. A perfect death. At least for Manu and me. But we weren't the ones who were dying. I hooked him up to an IV of glucose, and he came back to us.

Ciccio arrived the next morning to draw blood. He returned in the late afternoon with, by now, predictable tidings: Giovanni had to go immediately to the hospital. Manu and I were ambivalent. "What's the point?" we were both thinking. Why not just let him die in his own home, surrounded by the things with which he feels comfortable and the people whom he loves? We told Ciccio our hesitations, but he strongly believed that in the hospital Giovanni could recover sufficiently to make it worthwhile. In addition, he advised us, there would be the problem of caring for Giovanni at home as well as the impact that it could have on Zach and Stefano. We consented, but throughout the remaining five weeks of Giovanni's life, we constantly went back and forth on our position. What was the point, after all? Once, we sought the advice of the hospital's psychologist. She asked us one simple question that humbled us instantly. "Why not ask Giovanni what he wants?" The three of us walked through the ward to Giovanni's room. I climbed on the bed and whispered to Giovanni the possibilities—home, a private clinic, the hospital—and what they would entail in the simplistic language one uses with a small child. To our surprise, Giovanni replied, "I want to stay here."

During the course of the afternoon, there had been a slow and unusually large accretion of visitors to the apartment: Silvia, Manu, Donatella, Manu's daughter Sara. I dreaded telling Giovanni that he had to return to the hospital. I went into the bedroom and crouched over him. "You have to go into the hospital again. Which one of us would you like to go with you? Your mother is here, your sister is here, I am here. Whomever you want." He asked me to go with him. Ciccio called the ambulance while I packed Giovanni's bag again. When the ambulance arrived, the sirens drew an enormous crowd of people below our living room window. Four paramedics entered the apartment carrying a stretcher that resembled a large sheet loosely draped over two poles. Giovanni was placed into it, and he sank beyond view, tiny, in a cocoon. He asked to be covered with his down coat and an orange Sabena Airlines coverlet that he had once taken during his peripatetic days as a journalist. As the paramedics made their way with the stretcher through the dining room to get to the hall, they brusquely shoved aside the large dining room table in order to make room. All the family members were in the dining room having individual reactions that ranged from fretful nail-biting to hysterics. In the midst of the chaos, I took Zach aside to explain to him that I was taking Papa to the hospital and that I would be back very soon. When we reached the sidewalk, we could barely get through the crowd. Above us, Zach was hanging out of the window screaming, "Daddy, Daddy!!" with a look of horror on his face that has tattooed my soul.

I accompanied Giovanni in the back of the ambulance. The windows had been covered entirely by decals, and the careening movement as we made our way through the streets of Rome was nauseating. The sound of the siren was hollow in this small, padded space. I held Giovanni's hand. "Water, water," was all he would say.

At the hospital, I asked to speak to the doctor in charge of the AIDS ward. He arrived a half hour later and I explained to him that Giovanni was not to take any medications except those we had brought back from Switzerland. He smirked and said, "And I'll bring my magic wand tomorrow." Then he walked away.

After waiting in the corridor of the admissions area for more than an hour, during which time I gave him fourteen glasses of water, Giovanni was finally taken to the familiar ward, though this time he was given a semi-private room with only one roommate. Once he was in bed and asleep, I made my way to the head nurse, with whom by now I had a good relationship. I explained to her our decision not to use any traditional medications and gave her instructions as to how and when to administer the Rovirax and the injection. She wrote the instructions down in her book and assured me that it would be taken care of.

The next morning, I asked Giovanni if he had received the Swiss medications. His response, by now a frequent one: "I don't remember." I went back to the head nurse. "I'm sorry, but no medications are allowed to be brought in from the outside," she told me as if the conversation of the previous night had never taken place. Since the oral medications were easy enough to administer, I decided to hide them in Giovanni's drawer and administer them myself. As far as the twice-a-week injection, I decided to prepare it at home, bring it to the hospital, take Giovanni in the bathroom, and administer it there.

There wasn't the slightest hint of improvement. After a few days of intravenous feeding, Giovanni was, at most, able to read for five minutes. Then he would drop the newspaper in his lap, as if he had been holding an ingot of gold, and stare into space. Within a week, he was no longer able to control his bladder. A catheter was inserted with a tube that led to a bag that was fastened to the side of his bed, thus eliminating the possibility of my taking him to the bathroom for his injections. Shortly after, he became incontinent.

The doctors were either aloof or unobliging. They took every opportunity to remind us that by permitting Giovanni to be released from the hospital when we did, we had taken three years off his life. They rarely spoke to us, and even the nurses seemed to be in cahoots with the doctors. When I'd arrive at the hospital in the morning after taking Zach to school, Giovanni's diaper would be overflowing with diarrhea, his breakfast lying cold on his tray at the foot of the bed (surely they knew that he couldn't eat by himself, let alone push the tray, which didn't have wheels, up to his chest?!), various vitamins and mineral tablets still encased in their gauze wrappings on his night table.

Manu and I decided that, if only for purposes of rudimentary hygiene and care, it was necessary for someone to stay with Giovanni twenty-four hours a day. I did the first shift, from 9:00 a.m. until 4:00 p.m. The remaining time was divided among Manu, her daughter Sara, her friend and masseuse Simonetta, as well as Silvia, Flaminia, and Francesco, the latter coming to Rome from Milan every week for three or four days. Each afternoon after I'd return home from picking Zach up at school directly from the hospital, Manu and I would coordinate the next day's shifts, making sure that each person knew whether he or she was to bring lunch or dinner (after one week, Giovanni had refused to eat the hospital food) and whether he or she was arriving at a time when Giovanni needed a dose of the Swiss medication. We also kept a notebook in the drawer of his night table so that we could leave messages and general status reports: "Silvia, please try to get someone to inflate the air mattress when the beds are changed in the morning." "Manu, please call Flaminia and ask her to bring plastic cups and gloves. We're almost out." "Flaminia, we need to keep Giovanni's diapers open whenever possible, to let air in. He's getting a severe rash." "Sara, don't use the cream anymore, Giovanni's skin needs to breathe." Etc.

Within a few weeks, the night shift proved to be too strenuous for us, and we hired a nurse. This gave us greater flexibility, for now there were six of us to fill in the hours between 9:00 a.m. and 10:00 p.m. when the nurse arrived. I continued to stay in the hospital from 9:00 a.m. until 4:00 p.m., sitting quietly by Giovanni's side, always making sure that there was some physical contact between us amidst the silence and the gulf that separated us. We stared at each other for long stretches, we kissed, we rested together, head against head. Finally, we had our "white room."

15

March 23

At the hospital, sitting next to Giovanni's bed, I am comforted. His body is cadaverous, his mind is elsewhere, preparing itself for the ultimate conquest—or defeat or reconciliation. Each day he is further and further away from me; he is severing attachments to his history and settling somewhere else, solitary but tranquil. Yet, at the hospital, sitting next to Giovanni's bed, I am comforted. He is all these things. But he still is.

"I'll have to become a prostitute," he says in a barely audible whisper this morning, his "non sequitur du jour."
"Why?" I ask.
"To make money," he replies.
"We don't need to make more money. You're still receiving your salary from *L'Espresso*, I still have my income from the apartment building in Brooklyn, and we have some money in the bank."
"But that is a secret."
"Why is it a secret?"
No response.
"You can't become a prostitute, Gio. We love each other. And besides, we're married."

"We are?"

I lift his hand out from under the sheet, lace my fingers through his, and raise them up to his eyes to let him see our wedding bands. Then I dig into my backpack which lay by his bedside, retrieve the wedding invitation that I keep in a leather folder along with several choice photographs and Giovanni's original letter to me and show it to him as I describe to him our wedding day. He smiles, entranced, like a child being read a fairy tale.

"Do you remember it?" I ask.

"Remember what?"

"Our wedding."

"No."

March 24

He is going away from me, toward something or someplace else where the living have no right of entry. He is shedding his world, layer by layer, and one day, not too far away I fear, I will enter his room, and he will no longer know who I am. I am tempted today to ask him if he knows my name, but fear keeps me mute.

"I don't need to be part of a group. I don't need anybody," he says.

"Do you need me?"

"No."

The response rends me, but I want confirmation, clarification. "If I walked out of here right now and never came back, it wouldn't matter to you?"

"No."

I slowly withdraw my hand from his chest, traveling the rough terrain of his breastbone and upper ribs. As soon as the physical connection has been broken, he gleans my despair and looks toward me, then into my eyes, but somehow never at me. "You don't understand what I mean," he says. I don't reply. I understand what he means. I'm just not ready to hear it, to live it. I'm not ready to be unmerged from Giovanni as he tries, with the little effort he has remaining, to make his journey in peace, which requires a constant relinquishing of all that he has come in contact with. I am not ready for him to let go of me. I cling to him, wanting to accompany him as far as possible. I want him enveloped by me when he dies, in the way that he was the night we returned from Switzerland.

March 25

A desert storm from the Sahara pushes into Italy. The sky has a brownish glow, is too luminous, apocalyptic. The rain absorbs the dust and pelts every outdoor surface, covering all of Rome and its people in an ochre film. Giovanni is neutral, lumpen, wanting a presence, but a silent one. I decide not to talk, not to inspire, not to engage him. Nor do I touch him constantly, as in the past when I always held his hand, cupped my palm over his head, splayed my fingers across his chest. I am there but to myself. It is against the emotional grain, this forced unfastening; it is a letting go for both of us, for me from what has been my emotional center, for him from what is beckoning him to try to live just a bit more.

Martha, Giovanni's New York therapist of mythic proportions, arrives. She consoles, gives welcome advice, legitimizes our pain with professional strokes. I invite her to stay with me. If she says no, I will beg her to stay with me. She accepts. I tell her about the night that would have been his perfect death. She responds, "If Giovanni should die alone, at night, in the hospital, keep in mind that maybe he needs to be alone in order to die, that he doesn't want to be surrounded by those that call him to life." An elusive concept, but one that I am unable to ignore more and more each day. Letting go in small stages, for all of us. Giving up the permutations of control. She advises me to not "live" in the hospital, to pull back a bit, to take my own life back gradually.

March 26

Following Martha's advice. I give myself three hours today, not arriving at the hospital until 12:30. Unstructured time. Restless silence. Tides of grief crashing against my walls. At noon, I dash to the 719 bus. I need his company in my solitude, and I pretend that this need is reciprocal.

New instructions: Giovanni must now be turned every hour, like a roast, to prevent his bed sores from growing and deepening. His roommate's buttocks look like old kilns. At present, Giovanni's are a newborn pink. His calves are scaly, his hands bluish, his eyelids membranous. He looks reptilian.

Manu and I must fend off the friends and nonimmediate family members, who don't realize that Giovanni wants only a quiet presence, no conversation, news, etc., that their visit must be egoless, one in which they aren't coming to prove they are capable of bringing a smile to Giovanni's lips or a bout of vigor or nostalgia. He is past that now. He is veering away from the shapes and objects and noises and thoughts of life and toward a complete, unpeopled silence. Life is now the enemy.

March 27

Zach spends the night at Giovanna's. I go to Manu's concert and out to dinner afterward. Thank you, Martha. Martha speaks to Giovanni directly about death. "You are dying, Giovanni. You know that. Nothing matters. Words don't matter. We are losing you. You aren't losing us. You are going on. We are staying behind."

I invite a new friend, Sandro, and his young son, Michele, to the house this afternoon. Slowly carving out a life of my own, filling in the spaces left by Giovanni's continual shrinking, withdrawing from the habit of pain. Thank you, Martha.

Silvia and Francesco now accept that Giovanni is dying. No more tests, tubes, exams, proddings, pokings. Let him die with dignity, they say, echoing Manu's and my already obsolete revelation of two weeks ago. They insist on canceling the rectoscopy scheduled in two days. Manu and I had canceled it once. Now it is Silvia's turn. Waves of ambivalence. How to let Giovanni die? If no tests, then why continue with antibiotics, Bactrim, I/Vs, blood tests? Where does one draw the line? Francesco is feeding the fragile Silvia his own ambivalence, his own suffering, his own advice from a distance. He hangs up the phone and she is left with a double burden. Manu and I want the "scopias" (recto- and gastro-) to take place. Each time they are canceled, it takes at least two weeks to reschedule them. Giovanni is dying of diarrhea; let them conduct the final invasive procedure and be done with it. We can't know what Giovanni wants and, as Manu and I have learned, our interpretations are always sifted through our personal suffering. We have done an about-face—from wanting to bring him home to wanting to keep him in the hospital, at least for the time being. And if he is in the hospital, we should follow the treatment recommended by the doctors. This is our latest veneer of security, and Silvia and Francesco are one step behind. I think it best to leave at least this one decision to the doctors. They have been consistent throughout our wanderings. Let them have this one.

March 28

"I think, at the beginning, it is a sexual exchange on a higher level," Giovanni says.

"What is?" I ask.

A modulation in expression from deep in the cauldron of thought to a rising back into the usual blankness.

"What is?" I ask again.

"I don't remember."

March 29

When I tell him that Martha and her friend Deirdre have left for the States, he looks bewildered. "Leaving for the States? But where are we?"

"We're in Rome," I reply. "We live on via Natale del Grande in Trastevere. Do you remember our beautiful apartment that your mother found us?"

He doesn't remember and doesn't seem to care, as if he were fed up with all the things he is constantly being reminded that he cannot remember.

"Where did you think we were?" I ask.

"I don't know. Reality keeps changing."

"Reality keeps changing for all of us. That's what makes it so exciting. Try not to be afraid of the changes or upset by them. Relax and enjoy the unexpected. We're here with you on your journey. I was with you in New York, or Fire Island, in Rome. I am your traveling companion, as are your mother, father, Manu, Flaminia, Stefano, and Zach. OK?" I smile.

"OK." He smiles and falls asleep. I stop smiling.

March 30

Another gray brisk day. Giovanni is in an unhappy place today, or perhaps there is some physical pain that makes periodic jabs in his closed-eyed world. Occasionally, he moans, but he will not open his eyes or speak. If his eyelids begin to lift, revealing a sliver of red-threaded cornea, he shuts them again. Something about him today is sullen and inconsolable. I wash down his face, arms, legs; massage his limbs and extremities and exercise his legs, bending them toward his chest as I describe to him a country walk. His extremities are bluish, his nails brittle, the arc between his thighs vast. This afternoon I will try to massage his buttocks. Why? He is dying. He will never be restored. So why the fuss? I'm not sure. Maybe one simply can't do nothing.

Last night, I didn't take sedatives before going to sleep. I am becoming accustomed to an unshared bed. It has been five weeks since Giovanni lay in our bed, with the exception of the night of the perfect death. There is now a long chapter between the solitary bed and the one in which an ardent couple tousled between sheets. During the past five weeks, I've found myself moving away from "my" side of the bed, ever closer to the center. The bed no longer has sides. It is mine.

I ask Giovanni to take my hand to where it hurts. First, he places it on his abdomen, the unstoppable fount of his diarrhea where all hope of energy is mangled and pureed twenty-five times a day into a green and viscous River Styx. Then he puts my hand near his heart, pressing my knuckles into it with a pressure that makes me fear I will crush his catheter. The hurt in the abdomen, I understand. It is a single arrow. The hurt of the heart is a quiver of arrows, and each is its own messenger of pain. I choose not to choose one.

March 31

Gella, Manuela, Carmen, Paolo, and Fiamma call to hear how Giovanni is and to ask when they can come to visit him in the hospital. I have to tell them not to come, that Giovanni is trying to die, and they are part of life, that they will push him inadvertently in the wrong direction. Manu, Silvia, and I are no longer a part of life for Giovanni. We are the characters in his slow passage away from life. Others are disruptions, roadblocks to his journey. How to explain this to them without making it sound like we are holding Giovanni captive? Everyone seems to understand. At least they comply. Sometimes I wonder if I am holding Giovanni captive, whether it is I who cannot cope with the people who comprised his active, healthy life. They evoke the asymptomatic Giovanni, and this image is my greatest source of grief. In them, I harbor a retrospective jealousy for all the years they had with Giovanni. At this point, however, he doesn't respond to anyone. I know that he recognizes me, but in exactly what way, I am not sure. Does he know that I am Brett, his companion? Or does he recognize me simply as that sweet, attentive person who spends a lot of time with him each day in the hospital? As long as Giovanni does not talk in a way that makes sense to us, which will probably be until he dies, this identity crisis (of his? of mine?) will never be understood.

April 1

I spoke with Silvia last night, and much to my surprise, she brought up the subject of funeral arrangements. I had expected this to be a topic to be discussed between Manu and me. We are in agreement that a Jewish burial would be most appropriate. Giovanni grew up in Rome and returned to Rome; he was born of a Jewish mother and recently returned to Judaism. A Jewish burial would bring him full circle in this sphere of his life. Silvia's grandparents are buried in the Jewish section of a cemetery in Rome, Verano, which Silvia says is lovely. She will make inquiries about availability in the family plot, and I will find out about rabbis, minyans, and other essentials. I had a vivid, realistic dream about Giovanni's funeral. He had died in the hospital, and I arrived in time to watch him being zipped up inside what looked like a clear plastic suitor. We were trying to figure out where to keep him until the funeral arrangements could be made and decided on the terrace, as we had with Moats, where Zach wouldn't see him. I couldn't shake the dream off during the day.

Today, Giovanni has the much-dreaded gastroscopy. The doctor permits me to be with him. I hold Giovanni's hand and, while the doctor snakes a twelve-foot black hose down his throat, whisper into his ear a long story about a stroll in the country and along the beach. With the exception of a two-second bout of choking, Giovanni seems to be completely relaxed, and the procedure is over in about five minutes. The diagnosis? What I'd expected: nothing. It's always the same good news—nothing—yet there he is, dying. Strange, this consistent blind spot of the doctors. The rest of the afternoon he is a bit restless, his breathing shallow and irregular. The right eye, from which a contact lens had been extracted several days ago after floating in his eye for two weeks, seems to be growing weaker. It droops and doesn't follow the left eye. Watching Giovanni's blank stare and unresponsiveness, I begin to wonder whether perhaps the CMV is beginning to make incursions into his eyes and/or brain. I will make inquiries tomorrow. (Why?) The doctor who performed the gastroscopy recommends that Giovanni not eat solid food for "a while," as its nutritional value is negligible given the fact that he is on I/Vs of nutrients twenty-four hours a day, and solid food only exacerbates his diarrhea. I expected this development and was already wondering why we were going to the trouble of preparing all of Giovanni's meals at home and then coordinating their delivery, when Giovanni never eats more than one or two forkfuls and, even then, without particular relish. I am relieved in one respect: my mornings are now simplified. I no longer have to prepare a hot lunch during the forty-five minutes I have between waking up and getting Zach to school. And yet I see this development as, at best, the next-to-last one before Giovanni dies. The only change that remains, and it is one that isn't a prerequisite to death, is for Giovanni not to recognize us at all. And this is something we'll never be sure about anyway. It is conceivable that that is the case right now.

While massaging Giovanni this morning, I notice several black threadlike lines along his arms. The nurse informs me that these were caused by two blood transfusions that were given to him the night before, for which his veins were jabbed six times because four of the veins broke in mid-transfusion. And then this evening, I discover that the nurses tried to use a pump to extract the mucus from Giovanni's lungs but Giovanni refused. The mucus is beginning to collect rapidly; his cough is more and more persistent, and his teeth and corners of his mouth are coated with a clear gel. How ugly does it have to get?

I wish I could bring him home and let him die quickly. But there is no guarantee that he would die quickly or peacefully. And so, I keep vigil. Hurry, please. Hurry.

April 9

It has taken me six days to be able to write the following words: Giovanni died. The morning after Tuesday's gastroscopy, Silvia called me to tell me that Ana, our private night nurse, had called to tell her that Giovanni had had difficulty breathing during the night and had been put on oxygen. I rushed Zach to school, only to find out that the school would be closed from Thursday afternoon until the following Wednesday because of elections, and then made my way to the hospital. I opened the door and saw Giovanni hooked up to a large green tank that emitted oxygen through a cylindrical tube of water and then up through another accordion tube that attached itself to a mask covering Giovanni's nose, mouth, and chin. It was not an unfamiliar scene. A patient in the next room had been hooked up to an oxygen tank for several weeks. I remember thinking when I first saw this extremely young prey, "I'll find a way to let Giovanni die before he ever has to wear one of those." And there he was, wearing one of these life-sustaining devices that made me ask, "What kind of life is it sustaining?" And yet I made no move to have it taken off. Its presence violated his dignity. Its absence would deprive him of oxygen. How to weigh the two? Strange how one's resolve, forged over weeks and weeks, can slip away like mercury. Giovanni was physically and mentally unresponsive, though his eyes were half-open. His breathing was shallow and required great effort, perhaps all of his effort.

After the doctors made their morning rounds, I asked them about his condition. For the first time, they abandoned their usual nattering about levels of this and that and, seeming to finally recognize that here was a human being and not a composite of counts and ratios, stated simply—and rather obviously—that the situation was extremely serious. Giovanni had had a collapse. He was dying. There was essentially nothing that could be done. The time frame? "Poco," was all they would say. I decided to spend the night at the hospital and the next night and however many it would take for Giovanni's body to yield. I would make the funeral arrangements from the pay phone down the hall. And Zach? Who would take care of him since he had no school? One day at a time.

Zach returned home from school that Wednesday with a fever, which, by the time I had given him dinner, played with him, and gotten him ready for bed, had risen to 104 degrees. I was torn: should I spend the night with my feverish child or with my dying spouse? My friends Marina and Bernhard agreed to spend the night and the following morning with Zach until I was replaced at the hospital by Silvia and could come home. When I arrived back at the hospital at 10 o'clock that evening, the oxygen mask had been taken off. The nurse told me that it was best not to keep it on uninterruptedly so that Giovanni wouldn't absolutely depend on it. "How will I know if he needs to have it put back on?" I asked. "Believe me, you'll know," she said. As it turned out, Giovanni spent the entire night without the mask. I was almost hopeful about this microchange in his condition. Almost. Manu was going to spend the second night with Zach, though she vehemently disagreed with my decision to leave Zach in order to return to the hospital to spend the night with Giovanni. I cried. It was the first time that Manu and I didn't see eye to eye on something and it couldn't have come at a more difficult moment. Giovanni remained unresponsive throughout the night, and by the morning, his cough worsened; he sounded as if he were drowning in his own sputum. The oxygen mask was put back on, which restored his regular, shallow breathing for about an hour. Then the coughing started again. Giovanni's mother and father arrived in the morning, and I decided to dash home to find a replacement for Manu so that the two of us could return to the hospital.

When I arrived home, Manu was serving lunch—orecchiette with broccoletti—to Zach, and as she was ladling out the food, the phone rang. It was Giovanni's father. It was 12:30. Giovanni was dead.

Giovanni died with his mother and father at his side, gripping his hands and arms, stroking his forehead. Three individuals who had become estranged from one another over the years, finally reunited and reconciled, not through years of therapy or epistolary intimacy or long-distance telephone conversations, but through a moment as primordial as giving birth. As Martha had said, "Words don't matter."

16

Bicycling from our home in Monteverde to a friend's house in Flaminio for lunch, my four-year-old son, Zach, and I reached Trastevere, the neighborhood where the three of us—Giovanni, Zach, and I—lived when we moved to Rome seventeen months ago. As we started to make our way over the Ponte Garibaldi on that brisk winter afternoon, Zach perched on the molded plastic seat mounted in front of mine, I looked out at the dome of the synagogue and started mentally alighting on various pit stops in the future: should I send Zach to a Hebrew school when he finishes *asilo* next year, should I try to write some articles on anti-Semitism in Italy for an American magazine, when will I feel a tinge of homesickness for New York, is there time to stop at the pasticceria in the Ghetto and buy an American-style cheesecake to bring to lunch...

"Daddy, Giovanni is dead." Zach's words were scooped up by the strong breeze from the Tiber and hurled into my face. My simple reveries dissolved like a dream obliterated by the shrill command of an alarm clock. Wake up. Face the day. Get out from under the warm blanket. Face it. Face it. There we were, father and son, crossing the Tiber on a bicycle, clear Sunday air and honeyed morning light illuminating a panoramic tableau of serenity. Yet the spoken detail shatters all, and for an instant, it is one year ago. We are still on the Ponte Garibaldi. Zach is nestled on Giovanni's lap. Giovanni is sitting in his wheelchair. I am guiding the awkward vehicle along the street. We are on our way to Piazza Navona for La Befana. I know that by the time we reach the Piazza, my hands will be raw from negotiating the wheelchair over the cobblestones. And they are. Giovanni has been gathering his energy for this family outing for two weeks. But despite the crowds, the uproarious commotion, he is fast asleep upon arrival.

And after this instant, there is another in which the litany of the past year is repeated once more: I can't believe Giovanni is dead. I simply can't swallow this stuff, this bitter portion. It cannot be. And yet it is, and I know that for the rest of my life, I'll carry this dull ache, this nauseating breathlessness, because he IS dead and nothing about that can be changed, and nothing can replace his absence, that there is and always will be this space, this pregnant void that resists being filled by anything other than the fact of his total and incomprehensible absence.

"Yes, honey. Giovanni is dead." There is silence. I want to close the door but I must keep it open, for Zach. I must understand how his young mind is processing this formidable experience. Even here, in the midst of a tranquil outing, images of death aren't rebuffed. Zach is working hard. I must encourage him. "I miss Giovanni. Do you?" I ask.

"Oh, yes, Daddy. I cried when he was sick. But then he went into the hospital, and they made him better." He speaks with authority as if he is the one with the mission to inform, to console. I want to modify his interpretation, bring it closer to the truth, but how much closer, and with what words and concepts? What, after all, did I experience that Zach didn't? He saw me administer Giovanni's medications through the catheter that had been inserted in Giovanni's stomach during the first of four hospital visits; he saw Giovanni's blood being drawn twice a week at home by a nurse; he watched me empty Giovanni's portable urinal each morning; he accompanied us to Switzerland for an experimental treatment that failed; he watched Giovanni being taken away in an ambulance; he went to the funeral; the only thing Zach didn't witness was when Giovanni was dead. This is the only piece of the tragedy I spared him—Giovanni smiling in his hospital bed, his papery skin cooling and stiffening beneath my touch—the only episode that I kept out of his reach. Did I give Zach an overdose of reality? Or was it right and healthy that he should bear witness to the process, the evolution of death? I had been at Giovanni's side almost constantly from the time that his symptoms began, observing the facets of his gradual erosion with the scrupulousness of a scientist, although it was far from dispassionate. And yet when the facial muscles relaxed into a permanent expression of sublime relief, when the smile started to freeze, when the heart stopped beating, when he had crossed over, it was not the next, and final, step. In fact, it had nothing whatsoever to do with everything that had preceded it. It was a quantum leap, entirely other. With all my microcare and micro-observation, what, after all, do I really know that I can offer to Zach?

But the door must remain open. "Do you know where Giovanni is now, Zach?"

"He's still in the hospital."

"No, sweetie. Giovanni isn't in the hospital. He's in a very special place. A lot of people call the place Heaven. Some people think it is way up in the sky. I'm not sure where it is. It's certainly so far away that we won't be able to see him. But the most important thing is that in this place Giovanni feels all better and is very, very happy. And that makes me happy."

Before Zach can respond, a large truck turns into our lane. It is a street cleaner, Zach's favorite. I know that his attention and curiosity will now be veered away from the subject at hand and to the marvel of the enormous rotary brushes sucking up garbage and spraying water. I am relieved. I've rehearsed a zillion variations of this conversation in my head, patched together from books, therapy, friends, intuition. And yet none seems satisfactory. I suppose because what I want to achieve is impossible: to make the untimely death of a loved one seem OK. It is not OK. It is inordinately sad.

My life stopped in its tracks when Giovanni died. A year has passed. Contrary to my expectations, Zach and I are still in Rome. Giovanni's family has become our family. We have our friends, our routine. Days at school and at work, evenings at home alone or with friends, weekends in the park or the countryside, an occasional "adult" night out for me. There is variety, balance, stability, happiness, much the way I imagine it would have been had we been three instead of two. But the emotional tenor is so remote, so contradistinctive to that of a year ago as if its melody is being sung in a different key. This "new" happiness still does not fit.

Every so often, Zach proffers one of his seemingly impromptu remarks about Giovanni's death, for which I am unable to make any associative link. Each time, I realize how hard Zach is working and, by my own startled reaction and fluttering breath, how hard I am working to push it away, for there is no making sense out of it. Like Giovanni, I too, lived fast, took risks. I looked askance at danger. And, like him, I'm glad I did. I never need yearn for unspent youth. However, I cannot account for why some of us slipped through unharmed, intact. I want to grab my son and walk him through life and protect him with my very body, like a shield, from every conceivable harm. In him, I rediscover questions. And in him, I often find answers.

17

THE END OF THE WORLD IN ROME

The night before the end of the world, we stayed home since—not surprisingly—we weren't able to find a babysitter. We ended up watching the whole thing on television. I don't know that we were much worse off for that. Had we gone out, we could have partaken only of the happenings in the street of our neighborhood, which is rather dull to begin with. Staying in front of the screen, zapping the channels, allowed us to be aware of what was going on in the whole planet. Much more thrilling! Of course, one might argue that we could have taken our daughter out, like most people did, and that missing the experience of this particular night was really unforgivable. But she is funny about her bedroom rituals, and the last thing I wanted was to go around with a whining child in a throng of drunken thugs. Actually, as we saw on television, most people were drunk but didn't misbehave. Eighty percent of the police force showed up for work. They were dispatched to watch the luxury buildings where lavish parties were going on to keep the common folks from crashing them. But here and there they failed. An excited TV reporter stood in front of the Trump Palace in New York City, interviewing the people who were swarming in and out. A stout man with a Brooklyn accent said: "Champagne, and salmon, and caviar, and all the goods!" His companion shouted: "I'm wearing Gloria Vanderbilt's wig." She was also wearing a bracelet clearly taken from inside. The wig did nothing to improve her appearance. Her reddish, pock-marked face was flushed with vulgar delight.

On another channel, a talk show with Italian personalities was in progress. The debate had obviously started a while before. A thin, bald pundit with spectacles was vehemently arguing: "Where are you now, all you prophets of doom? Keeping a low profile, huh? There has been almost no breakdown of civility, except the riots in Rio de Janeiro, which was a city on the verge of collapse anyway, and the bombing of Israel, but that was a political decision, not the eruption of faceless crowds. A few beatings, less killings than on an average weekend night. Let's face it. The human race is saying farewell in a much more graceful way than the way it has lived." His opponent, a fat man with a red beard, barged in. "Absolutely not! Where's the grandness, where's the perception of tragedy? People are only interested in looting and gorging themselves on expensive food. And, of course, drinking. It's only material things. The ugly consumerism has finally infected the whole planet, and it's only fit that we end this way. Where are the speeches? Where are the attempts to make sense of this experience? Where's Moravia?" It was boring, and we turned channels. My wife excitedly shrieked: "Look! Look! That's my cousin-in-law!" I was annoyed by her usual imprecision. "What do you mean? There isn't such a thing." "Of course there is. He's my cousin Rita's husband or ex-husband." "In that case, he's your cousin." "No matter," she went on volubly, in striking contrast to her usual placidity. "I can swear it was him. He was standing with a group of people, and they were all shouting or singing, like this," and she shaped her mouth like an "O" to show me how her cousin's mouth was in that fateful moment. Exasperated, I went to the window, followed by her bubbly talk: "Can you believe it? Wait until I tell Rita! Oh, won't she be thrilled!" In the concrete interior courtyard, I could see a pathetic attempt at a party. In a conga line that was going back and forth, I could make out the accountant from the third floor and the couple next door with whose ugly and stupid daughter our own daughter sometimes plays. Their little monster was down in the courtyard too with the other children from the building, permitted at last to go into the flowerbeds and bring about that destruction they'd always wished for. I closed the window. My wife was still talking about her family, and I decided it was time to pull out the champagne, the very expensive bottle I had purchased that afternoon. She was delighted. She couldn't believe her eyes. Her face broke out in red patches. I poured the wine in the flute glasses—finally, some of those wedding presents came in useful!—and while we were drinking, the atmosphere in the room perceptibly changed. The air was suffused with a glow that didn't come from the TV screen. I started making passes at my wife, half-jokingly, half-seriously. She was awkward at first, then she seemed to enjoy the flirtation. In that moment, our daughter woke up, screaming.

My wife hurried into her bedroom and came out again right away with an accusatory expression. "Her elephant! You forgot her elephant!" She grabbed the stuffed animal and went back in, and soon her loving and cooing whispers made our daughter fall back asleep. I didn't even try to help, knowing too well that that would only have redoubled her hysterics.

My wife came back and sat on the sofa, dejected. The spell was broken, and we resumed watching TV. I don't know what had happened between us. I was still quite fond of her, but no more than you might be of an old-maid sister who takes care of you. I don't think it was her having had a baby that made her less sexual in my eyes. Rather, I was jealous of the relationship between her and the girl, that easy intimacy I could never attain.

The TV screen was a blur of rapidly changing images

and voices. The remote was in my wife's hands. Unlike me, she enjoys zapping quickly through the channels. A masculine characteristic, I'm told. But I could make out enough from what we were seeing. The look of forced gaiety on people's faces had given way to a desperation and emptiness so entrenched that one couldn't help thinking they long preceded the recent events. One channel was broadcasting, live from Vienna, a rendition of the Heroic Symphony. I convinced my wife to settle on this show, and she fell asleep quietly on the green sofa next to me. After a while, her head slid to the side and she started snoring lightly, a veil of saliva over her mouth.

The next morning, the portentous breakdown of civilization had occurred. Nobody showed up for work, except for a few TV cameramen. All they could do was to give us a still image of some talking head with none of the theatricals to which we had grown accustomed. Our daughter wanted to go outside, so we took a stroll in the neighborhood. The pavement was littered with smashed objects, even furniture, and many toilet bowls as it is done in my country on New Year's Eve. Totally oblivious, our daughter headed straight to her favorite playground. There was a group of her girlfriends there, all dressed up in frocks and ribbons, and we felt ashamed of the plainness of her clothes. But the girls didn't mind, and soon they were busy jumping rope. The mothers, who usually mingled and chatted good-naturedly of inconsequential things, sat apart, mute, each next to her husband. Maybe it was this rare male presence that chilled the air.

After lunch, my wife wanted to defrost the refrigerator. I tried to convince her that it was pointless, but in the discussion, she grew more and more heated. "Don't you see?" she whined. "It's the same attitude of those people who didn't collect the garbage, who didn't show up for work. Only if we keep doing what's right, there is a chance . . . there is a chance . . ." And she burst into sobs, her head between her arms on the scratched surface of the kitchen table. Our daughter went to kiss her knee to comfort her while throwing me an accusatory side glance.

"All right, all right," I said, "Let's defrost the fridge. Maybe, while we're at it, we could also repaint the living room?"

My wife smiled through tears and set off to work, absent-mindedly humming a happy tune. We had been invited to spend the night at our next-door neighbors', but we declined. After a painful phone call from my mother-in-law, I convinced my wife that it was best to unplug the phone. Our daughter was taking an unusually late and long nap, which was good since I planned to keep her awake that night. The time seemed to solidify like gelatin. Each time I looked at my watch, the hands were always in the same position as before. Our daughter woke up in a cranky mood, but when I yelled at her, she didn't cry. She sat on her little chair sucking from her tippy cup and staring at me with big, scared eyes. The mood on TV was vastly different from the night before. Now it was mostly ministers and rabbis and imams. There was a Catholic priest thundering and urging us to repent for our sins. It was ugly and fascinating at the same time. Much more disturbing was a human sacrifice broadcast from Mexico. TV, I mused, had finally reached its ultimate essence—probably in that very moment there was some producer jumping up and down from happiness. We settled on cartoons to keep our daughter quiet. But by ten o'clock, all the stations had died, and we just couldn't keep her awake. With the little girl spread between us on the sofa, her chest rising gently and regularly, the two of us looked at each other awkwardly. I knew that something needed to be said that would rise to the occasion, sum up our life, express some superior belief, but all I could utter was: "You've been a good wife." Looking at me with moist eyes, she answered, "And you've been a good husband." We stayed on the sofa so we wouldn't wake up our daughter. From time to time, I stroked my wife's hands. We just sat there together, waiting.

—Giovanni Forti, Fire Island, August 1991

THE END

About the Author

BRETT SHAPIRO is an American writer and the author of three novels: *Henry's Version* (2024), *Late in the Day* (2022) and *Those around Him* (2019). His best-selling memoir *L'Intruso* was originally published in Italy, where he lived for 25 years, and later became an award-winning film and theatrical production. He is the author of two children's books, one of which was the recipient of Austria's National Book Award. His short stories have been performed in theatres throughout Italy. He is a veteran writer for the United Nations and currently lives by the beach on Cape Cod and in Florida.

About Atmosphere Press

Founded in 2015, Atmosphere Press was built on the principles of Honesty, Transparency, Professionalism, Kindness, and Making Your Book Awesome. As an ethical and author-friendly hybrid press, we stay true to that founding mission today.

If you're a reader, enter our giveaway for a free book here:

SCAN TO ENTER
BOOK GIVEAWAY

If you're a writer, submit your manuscript for consideration here:

SCAN TO SUBMIT
MANUSCRIPT

And always feel free to visit Atmosphere Press and our authors online at atmospherepress.com. See you there soon!

www.ingramcontent.com/pod-product-compliance
Lightning Source LLC
LaVergne TN
LVHW041936070526
838199LV00051BA/2815